WHAT PEOPLE ARE

Gamma Healing is a wonderfully effective tool for personal growth, for it offers valuable insight for self-diagnosis, as well as a strategic plan to more effectively redefine the path of our evolutionary journey. I highly recommend Chris Walton's inspiring book as a guide for experiencing a life overflowing with peace, happiness and love.
Bruce H. Lipton, PhD, cell biologist and bestselling author of *The Biology of Belief: Unleashing the Power of Consciousness, Matter and Miracles*

In this really motivating, enjoyable and easy to read book Chris Walton shows you how to 'program' your brain-mind-body to create a successful life. It is cutting edge and is something we all need to know to help us live a happy and fulfilling life.
Kazadi K.N. Kalangu, MD, Brain Surgeon and Professor of Neurosurgery, Vice President of the World Federation of Neurosurgical Societies

Chris Walton has written an eye-opening, habit-changing, life-enhancing book. It deserves to be a bestseller.
Graham Hancock, Bestselling Author of *Fingerprints of the Gods and Supernatural*

Out of hundreds of books on personal development I have read, this book stands out from all the others. It is transformational and totally inspiring.
Vlatka Hlupic, Professor of Business and Management, University of Westminster, London

If you want or need to create lasting and profound change in any area of your life use this book. In my 19 years in the field of personal development there have been many authors promising the holy grail of positive lasting change which are mainly based on outdated positive thinking and motivational techniques. This book stands out above them all, in my experience this is the only one that really delivers!.

Alec Grimsley, bestselling author of *Vital Conversations*,
How to make the impossible conversation possible

This book changed my life—literally! My crippling fear of public speaking has been holding me back all my life. Having completed the belief-change process around my fear, I am now shaping my future around teaching and public seminars. I urge you not to miss this opportunity to transform your life.

Rhoda Kingston, BA, BSc, Naturopath

Understanding the power of your own mind is the most important thing any of us can do. Gamma Healing explains this with such clarity and encouragement. This book shows us that by updating our belief systems and expanding our consciousness we can remove our fears, doubts and worries and reprogram our whole being for a more fulfilling life. It is a sensational read.

Jeff Moran MA, Director, MindSounds,
www.Mindsounds.com

GAMMA HEALING

Eliminate Subconscious Limiting Beliefs,
Anxiety, Fear and Doubt in Less Than
5 Minutes

CHRIS WALTON MSc

First published in December 2010 as Incredible You – Unleashing the Power of Your Beliefs and Intentions to Achieve an Extraordinary Life. Retitled and published again as Gamma Healing on 11.11.11

© Chris Walton 2010
The right of Chris Walton to be identified as the author of this work has been asserted in accordance with the Copyright, Designs and Patents Act 1988.

ISBN: 978-0-9565527-0-9

British Library Cataloguing in Publication Data

A catalogue record for this book is available from the British Library.

Printed in the UK by Lightning Source.

CONTENTS

To the Incredible You...

Believe nothing because a wise person said it.

Believe nothing because a belief is generally held.

Believe nothing because it is said in ancient books.

Believe nothing because it is said to be of divine origin.

Believe nothing because someone else believes it.

Believe only what you test and judge to be true.

— Attributed to the Buddha

ACKNOWLEDGEMENTS

The idea for this book came to me during a time in my life of profound self-realisation. Many friends helped me through this transition. Maggie, thank you for an amazing, wild and transformational three years. Your kindness and ability to love have been a great teacher for me. You will always have a special place in my heart, Namaste.

Hawky, thank you for being there for me whenever I needed someone to put the white coat on and listen to my ramblings. You have helped me stay relatively sane for many years, my friend. I appreciate your wisdom and that bloody five pattern, thank you Mark.

Jonny Boy, thank you for helping me step on this path. Thank you for being there when I needed stability and somewhere to stay while I planned my next chapter, and thank you to all at Rhodes Mansions with two legs and four for letting me into your happy home.

Alec, thank you for making that call over ten years ago and your constant support, encouragement, wisdom and way of being. Andy Orange, thank you for our awesome conversations and deep connection. Jeffers, thank you matey for giving me the amazingly powerful MP3s (www.mindsounds.com) and being in my life. You were the first person I met that is truly with the programme. Dearest Charlie, thank you for being my friend, your spirit touches mine and everyone you meet. Oh yes, and thank you for that title idea you thought was crappy, hahaha. You are an angel and I'm glad this book is touched with your energy. Vee, thanks for your constant support and encouragement in all I do. You have a huge heart. Roysta, broski, over 30 years of top friendship, quality my man, quality, rage on.

Thank you to my course sponsors, Liz and Rodger in Scotland and Nenad, Jelena and Ana in Croatia. Thank you to Ole and Marjana in Slovenia who sponsor my courses in Slovenia and where the first chapter of this book was born—happy days! Thank you to Frank DeMarco, Nancy Dorman, Alec Grimsley, Graham Hancock, Professor Vlatka Hlupic, Professor Kazadi Kalangu, Rhoda Kingston and Charlotte Sinclair for your valuable feedback on the manuscript.

Thank you to Stephanie Burton for being the beautiful model for the belief-change photographs and spending the time to write your amazing entanglement story. Thanks to Bernard Chandler (www.graffik.co.uk) for the images, book cover design and fun conversations. A super huge thank you to Joan Parisi Wilcox, my dear friend and editor. Joan, thank you so much for playing such a big part in creating this book. You are an amazing person on every level and your writing and editing skills are from the gods. Thank you for transforming my manuscript into this wonderful, easy-to-read book. You are a rare, precious jewel and so very with the programme, from the bottom of my heart—thank you.

I would also like to thank my sister and brother-in-law, Julie and Roger, for their love and support from day one and my two nephews and friends, James and Edward, for being really cool dudes.

And of course, my dear little mum. Indeed, mum, good things do come in little packages, you did an amazing job.

Much love to you all.

FOREWORD

The information in this book is truly something we all need to know. Most people are educated—we might even say brain-washed—into believing they are not powerful beings and creators of their lives. However, because of research taking place at the leading edge of science today, we know this is not true and that indeed our brain–mind–body systems are all powerful when we know how to program them. That programming starts at the level of our most deeply rooted beliefs.

Beliefs determine who we are and what we receive from life. The life we are living right now, and what we have achieved so far, are a direct consequence of our deepest beliefs. Surprisingly, we often don't know what we really believe, for many of our thought patterns and belief programs remain hidden in our subconscious minds. Until now, it was difficult to access them, never mind to change them. The Mind–Body-Change Techniques that Chris Walton teaches do exactly that.

I first met Chris when I attended one of his workshops several years ago, and my life changed dramatically for the better. The techniques Chris taught to me and others are described in this book. They are easy to use, work quickly and, most importantly, give you the power to direct and tailor your own destiny. Every part of this book is substantiated by cutting-edge science, yet this information is explained with elegance, in an enjoyable and motivating style, making it accessible to everyone. These new Mind–Body Techniques grow out of Chris's years of research, teaching and coaching—and his passion to help people awaken to their true, innate potential. I was so impressed with this book that I have made it essential reading for all of my students. The information and techniques transformed me and my life—and I know it will transform you and your life as well.

Professor Kazadi Kalangu MD. Brain surgeon.
Vice President of the World Federation of Neurosurgical Societies.

PREFACE

The idea that thoughts, intentions and beliefs can affect our physical bodies, including our biology and physiology, has been the subject of inquiry since ancient times. Modern scientists who pioneered research into the mind's effect on the body or expanded on earlier theory range from Herbert Benson, Deepak Chopra, Mae-Wan Ho, James Oschman, Candace Pert, Rupert Sheldrake and Gary Schwartz to William Tiller, among many others. George Good heart and Roger Callahan were the early pioneers of what today is called 'Energy Psychology and Energy Medicine' on which the change techniques in this book are based. Laboratory research into how our mind affects not only our body but the world around us was conducted rigorously by Brenda Dunne, Robert Jahn and Roger Nelson and at the Princeton Anomalies Research Laboratory over a 30-year period. I would like to give a big thank-you to all these pioneers and visionary scientists and especially Dr Bruce Lipton, whom I have had the pleasure to be educated by since 2003. Dr Lipton's research massively enhanced my understanding of the hard science of the effects of the environmental signals and the mind on cell function and the impact of our beliefs on our biology. Dr Lipton's ground-breaking book *The Biology of Belief* has in part launched a near revolution in cell biology and the mind–body connection.

The Gamma Breakthrough

The Gamma Brain Technique© (which is part of the Gamma Belief Change Technique) has been scientifically validated by measuring brain wave activity using an E.E.G. This technique creates high levels of gamma brain waves in the genius centres of the brain – the frontal lobes. Gamma brain waves bind the brain together creating a peak state of consciousness. This is the ideal state to heal the body, eliminate fears, doubts and emotional stress and eradicate subconscious limiting beliefs.

INTRODUCTION

Your beliefs are the most powerful force in your mind and body. They massively affect every aspect of your life, from your wealth and finances to your health and fitness and the quality and passion of your love life. They can determine your failure or success, influence how you create and maximise opportunities and determine how you overcome challenges. They can even foster what seem to be miracles...

Every year, Australia hosts a 543.7-mile (875-kilometre) endurance race that winds from Sydney to Melbourne. Experts consider it to be among the world's most gruelling ultra-marathons. The race takes on average a week to complete and is attempted only by world-class athletes. The majority of these athletes are 30 years old or younger, and they are supported by a full medical crew of doctors, massage therapists and nutritional experts. The race receives so much attention and is so serious a sporting challenge that runners are funded in their training by the big sports companies.

In 1983, a 61-year-old potato farmer named Cliff Young showed up, dressed in overalls and wearing work boots, and signed up for—and received—a runner's number. To everyone's amazement, especially the athletes', he took his place at the starting line.

The press and athletes were beyond curious about whether Cliff was truly going to attempt to run the marathon. When Cliff assured them he was serious, many of the runners tried to dissuade him, telling him he was crazy and could never finish the race. Cliff is reported to have to replied:

> *Oh, yes I can. You see, I grew up on a farm where we couldn't afford horses or tractors, and the whole time I was growing up, whenever the storms would roll in, I'd have to go out and round up the sheep. We had two thousand sheep on two thousand acres. Sometimes I would have to run those sheep for two or three days. It took a long time, but I'd always catch them. I can run this race.*[1]

When they learned he was serious about running, the medical doctors stepped in to try to talk some sense into Cliff, concerned as they were that he would seriously injure himself or have a heart attack. They reminded him how exceptionally challenging this race was, not just physically but also mentally and emotionally. Cliff did not listen. And so the race began.

It became apparent from the start that Cliff had an odd style of running—more of a shuffle than a run. The other runners almost immediately left him behind.

Long ago the experts had worked out the best way to run an ultra-long-distance race. The received wisdom was to run for eighteen hours and then sleep or rest for six hours, alternating running and sleeping periods on the same schedule throughout the race. Cliff was not aware of this race strategy. He did not sleep. He simply shuffled along, at his strangely slow pace, all day and night, and on into the second day. Members of the press ran up to him to interview him, asking him about his tactic for the race, astonished as they were at his style and that he was not taking sleep breaks. Cliff assured them he intended to continue to the end of the race with no such breaks. And he did. And each day he got closer to the lead pack of racers—which included some of the world's top long-distance runners.

On the fifth night, Cliff crossed the finish line—first. He had run the race and won it in record time—five days, fifteen hours and a couple of minutes—beating the course record by two days! It was an amazing story: a 61-year-old potato farmer in boots and overalls shuffled his way to a record in one of the world's most gruelling races. How had he done it? Without a doubt, one reason for his success was his invincible belief that he could do it.

But there was also science behind his win. After studying Cliff Young's unusual running style, sports experts were forced to change their beliefs about the best strategy to run ultra-long-distance races. The preferred method became the 'Young Shuffle', for the sports physiologists discovered that the shuffling style Cliff used expended less energy than the traditional running style. This technique has been adopted by many ultra-marathon runners since, and at least three of the subsequent winners of the Sydney to Melbourne race have used the Young Shuffle to win.

★ ★ ★

Cliff's story is one about self-confidence, about his unshakeable belief in himself and his abilities. By all accounts—especially in the opinion of the sports and medical experts—Cliff should have failed, and failed miserably. But he defied all the odds. A sceptic might say that experience accounted for his success, not his belief in himself. After all, he had been running long distances on the farm since he was a boy, so perhaps it was not so unusual that he could pull off the marathon win. It may have been that his record-setting victory was a one-in-a-million occurrence, but it was not entirely out of the realms of possibility.

If you believe that Cliff's sheepherding experience or an energy-saving running style are the primary explanations for how he did what he did, instead of the power of his belief in himself, then read on. Here is a true account about the power of belief that defies any rational explanation.

Mr Wright had just hours to live. He had tumours the size of oranges throughout his body, his lungs were filled with fluid, his spleen and liver were enormously swollen, and he couldn't breathe without the help of supplemental oxygen. His physician, Dr Klopfer, had done everything he could using standard medical therapies to try to help Mr Wright—to no avail. Now that the end seemed near, Mr Wright was willing to consider non-standard treatments. One of these was a cancer drug, called Krebiozen, which, even though it was still undergoing clinical research, was being hailed by the popular media as a possible wonder cure for cancer. Dr Klopfer had access to the still-experimental drug, and when Mr Wright begged to be allowed to try it, Dr Klopfer agreed, even though doing so would go against medical protocol. He gained access to the drug and administered it to Mr Wright on a Friday, and then he left the hospital for the weekend, believing that Mr Wright would be dead by the time he returned on Monday. But when Monday came, Dr Klopfer was shocked to see Mr Wright up and walking around the ward, as if he had never been at death's door.

Tests were run, and the results were stunning—the tumours had shrunk to half their original size. Dr Klopfer continued the

Krebiozen treatments, and in less than two weeks Mr Wright was tumour free. Soon he was released from the hospital, returning home a healthy man.

A couple of months later, the media reported on the preliminary results of the clinical trials of this supposed wonder drug. The verdict: Krebiozen did not appear to be effective against cancer. Mr Wright heard these reports, and soon thereafter he felt unwell again. Examination revealed that his tumours were back. As his health deteriorated, he was readmitted to the hospital.

Dr Klopfer was at a loss to explain what was happening with Mr Wright. The dramatic disappearance of the tumours and their reappearance seemed to be more than a remission and relapse. He suspected that somehow Mr Wright's beliefs were involved, and that, in fact, those beliefs might be the strongest factor in what was happening. To test this theory, he gave Mr Wright injections of sterile water but told him that it was a 'new double-strength version' of the wonder drug Krebiozen.

Again, Mr Wright's tumours melted away, he regained his health, was released from the hospital and resumed his normal life. Shortly thereafter, there was a lot of press about an official report from the American Medical Association, the most respected and recognised medical professional organisation in the United States, declaring unequivocally that Krebiozen didn't work. In fact, one headline declared, 'Nationwide Tests Show Krebiozin to Be a Worthless Drug in the Treatment of Cancer'. Upon hearing this news, Mr Wright felt devastated, and, sure enough, a short time later his tumours reappeared and his health declined precipitously. He died two days after being readmitted to the hospital.

Dr Klopfer published a paper about his experience with Mr Wright, concluding that Mr Wright's optimistic beliefs appeared to be the main factor in the disappearance of his tumours and the regaining of his health, and the loss of that optimism and belief the main factor in their reappearance and Mr Wright's death.[2]

★ ★ ★

As this true story demonstrates, our beliefs are exceptionally powerful. And their power is pervasive, affecting us at every level of our being—from our moment-by-moment feelings about ourselves, to what we think we can achieve and accomplish, to what we expect to receive from those around us and to our perception of the state of the world at large. Our personal lives conform to our beliefs, and our world reflects back to us our collective beliefs. That's why the ancient mystical texts say, in many different ways, that we are not in the world, the world is in us. We, in effect, create the world through what we believe is possible and probable.

Belief is so powerful an agent of creation that it has become the subject of study in its own right. For example, as I will discuss later in this book, current science shows us that our beliefs strongly determine the amount of happiness, inner peace, optimism and other such qualities we experience, and influence our potential and how well we use our gifts and talents. Our beliefs largely determine the depth of connection we experience in our relationships and the level of success we can achieve in our work or creative endeavours. In fact, our thoughts and beliefs are so important to the state of our overall well-being that they are the object not only of psychological study but also of physiological, sports performance, medical and biological research. As leading neuroscientist Dr Andrew Newberg says, 'I have come to realise that the study of beliefs may be the single most important quest, both scientifically and spiritually.'[3]

★ ★ ★

We are at a unique time in human history, at a juncture where insights from quantum physics, the new biology and leading-edge psychology are joining forces to provide us with a deeper understanding of the mind–body relationship. The integration of this knowledge reveals to us our vast and powerful innate abilities—abilities as yet unrealised or untapped in most of us. Without overstating the facts, the evidence from the frontiers of research is that when we fully realise the power of our minds and expand our consciousness accordingly, our potential explodes, and is perhaps even limitless. Our beliefs are the measure of how much we can achieve, how exceptional we can be, how deeply we are fulfilled—and just about everything that determines who we are and the quality of our lives.

If you are sceptical about such claims, please read on. It is my intention in this book not only to educate you, but also to persuade you that changing and updating your beliefs is the most powerful and important thing you can do! I show you how to do this using techniques from the latest understanding of how the mind and the energy systems of the body function. These techniques will allow you to identify and then eliminate self-sabotaging patterns of belief and integrate empowering, goal-specific beliefs to assist you in creating the life you want.

As a performance psychologist, I specialise in change and performance improvement, and I have worked with thousands of people, in teams, groups and one on one, around the world. I have worked with organisations large and small and with world-champion athletes. I have seen the results attesting to lives changed and dreams realised by changing and updating belief systems. I share some of these testimonials at the end of this book. If you want to be inspired, I invite you to flip to the back of the book to read these stories from people just like you—regular people living regular lives with all the normal responsibilities, but who knew there had to be more to life and took the initiative to find out how to improve their lives. Quite literally, changing your beliefs is the fastest, most powerful and comprehensive way to improve your life.

Using the knowledge and techniques in this book you will remove subconscious limiting beliefs that have been hindering your potential and performance, perhaps for decades, perhaps for your entire life. I predict that you won't at first believe how easy it is to liberate your-self towards your fullest potential and deepest joy. Here's what I offer to you in this book:

❑ I will show you how to identify the beliefs that are holding you back, beliefs that are subconscious and so not even in your realm of awareness right now.

❏ I will show you how, working with and without a partner, you can release and reprogram these self-sabotaging subconscious beliefs in only one or two minutes each.

❏ I will show you how to completely release negative emotions from your mind–body in seconds, a release which for most people leads to huge increases in their mental, emotional and physical energies.

❏ I will share the leading-edge research and theory that underlie these change techniques and that will help you foster a new way of looking at the world.

❏ I predict that by using these techniques you will increase your success and attain greater levels of creativity, performance, happiness, love, health, wealth and whatever else you deem important in your life.

These techniques and processes are not primarily attitudinal; that is, they are not based on affirmations or positive-thinking processes. You certainly can practise positive thinking and use affirmations and motivational techniques to improve your confidence, performance or other aspects of yourself and your life, but in all likelihood you will achieve only short-term, transitory results. However, when you access your deepest, most fundamental and mostly subconscious self-defeating beliefs and repattern them, you achieve lasting and often profound change.

Are you ready? Ready to completely excise self-limiting thought patterns and belief systems from your mind–body and totally align yourself with a new reality of health, wealth, happiness, vitality and success? Then let's get started!

1

HOW DO YOUR BELIEFS AFFECT YOU?

The beliefs that we hold in our mind create the biology and behaviour of our lives.

Dr Bruce Lipton

You think you know what you believe, right? The fact is that most of us are driven by behaviours based on beliefs that we may not ever have examined, let alone agreed to hold. So let's get straight to the nuts and bolts of why you think, feel and act the way you do. The iceberg model illustrated in Figure 1 provides a simple metaphor that explains how beliefs influence our emotions and motivate our actions. As you know, an iceberg is approximately 90% unseen, submerged underwater, so we see only the tip of it. We can't really know how big it is or what it looks like. That iceberg is very much like beliefs—very few of them are conscious (above the water line of our knowing). Most remain hidden from us, submerged deep in our subconscious minds. We are not aware of what our unconscious assumptions and beliefs actually are, and yet they influence every aspect of our lives.

For now you can ignore the reference in Figure 1 to information and energy fields. We'll explore those in a later chapter. Just to be absolutely clear in our terminology: our behaviours are our actions (what we do, say etc.) and how we carry those actions out. Behaviours have a style that are encoded by beliefs, for instance by our world view and our personal style, which are things that can be generalised into 'types' (or even stereotypes). So, for example, some people are conservative, others liberal. Some are Type A personalities (outgoing, action oriented, extroverted) and some Type B (more retiring, introspective and introverted). Obviously what we do and say—and how we do and say things—strongly influence the outcomes of our interactions and the situations we create in our lives.

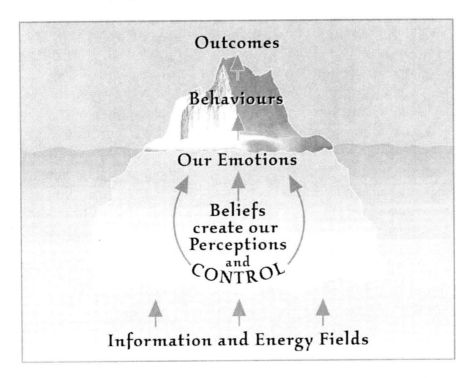

Figure 1 *Our beliefs create and control our perceptions. The way we perceive the world drives our emotional responses to events and interactions, which in turn governs the actions we take and ultimately has a large effect on the outcome of events and interactions.*

Our behaviours are driven by our emotions and feelings. (Some psychologists and other professionals make a distinction between emotions and feelings, but we won't split hairs here. I will use these terms interchangeably throughout this book.) We all know how powerful emotions can be: they can inspire us or paralyse us. When we feel confident, excited, appreciative, happy and full of vitality, we think and behave very differently from when we feel self-conscious, unsure, frustrated, stressed, tired or depressed. What we might not be aware of, however, is that many of the emotions we feel are determined by a deeper level of cause and effect—the level of our perceptions and beliefs. For example, if you express your opinion to someone and that person disagrees with you, you could feel many different emotions in response. You could simply accept that person has a different viewpoint and not feel much at all, because your underlying belief may be that everyone is entitled to his or her opinion. You could feel surprised that the person disagrees, and perhaps then feel frustrated that you may have been misheard. Your underlying belief is that the person is like you in many other respects and so should think like you. You might even feel self-righteous, feeling yours is the correct and logical opinion, and also feel dismissive of that person, thinking him or her ignorant or misguided. An underlying belief driving that response might be that there is a moral imperative behind the opinion and that any spiritual or ethical person would believe as you do. There are many possible responses because there are myriad beliefs that drive your emotional self. The point here is that to change our lives, we need to go deeper than simply exploring our emotions—we need to get to the level of our core beliefs. Emotions can be clues to our beliefs, but they are not enough in and of themselves to tell us what is really influencing us and our lives.

It's important to understand that I am not talking about attitudes here. Our overall emotional template is more than a set of attitudes. Attitudes, as in a positive versus a negative outlook on facing challenges and meeting opportunities, are important, but they are still surface level in terms of the impact they have on our lives, and they are subject to situation, environment, the people around us, and other transient influences. Beliefs go much deeper and form a more or less stable, even if unconscious, 'palette' by which we live our lives. The reality is that percolating beneath any of our core emotions is a set of conscious and subconscious beliefs that control our perceptions of life and thus also control our emotions, thoughts, and the quality of our actions and behaviours. The beliefs are the scaffolding that hold our emotions in place, however transient those emotions may be. Our beliefs are the foundation on which rests the entire structure of our life and its perceived quality.

Building on the definitions I have just given, I can go one step further and define beliefs in two primary ways, starting with the more scientific definition and moving to a more generalised and holistic one:

❏ According to many scientists and psychologists, a belief is any perception, cognition or emotion that the mind assumes, consciously or unconsciously, to be true.

❏ More generally, a belief is a thought or a collection of thoughts that determines a person's perceptions of the world and so influences, and even dictates, the choices that person makes, the relationships he/she has, the creations he/she manifests, the behaviours he/she demonstrates and ultimately the life that person lives.

The first definition, the one that is acceptable to most science-minded people, is not actually accurate in terms of 'change performance', for, as I have just explained, a belief is different to an emotion, and more foundational to our state of functioning. However, the part of that definition that I would like you to focus on and understand is the part about beliefs being what you believe 'to be true'. This idea will become important as we look more deeply at why your life looks the way it does right now and how you can change it if you so desire. The second definition is the one that I will be focusing on more intently in this book. I will be asking you to examine your core set of beliefs and how they are influencing you at the deepest level, as well as asking you to discern which of those beliefs are helping or hindering you in taking action, accomplishing your goals, socialising with others, healing your body, making sense of yourself and making meaning in your world.

For all the talk of emotions, thoughts and the unconscious and conscious aspects of the mind, beliefs are not only abstract things that have an impact on you psychologically. They exist in the form of thought patterns in your physical being. They are very real electrochemical signals that are broadcast throughout your body. They affect every aspect of your being, from your 'happiness factor' to the strength of your immune system, from your outlook on life to the cascade of your hormones, enzymes and overall body chemistry. Thoughts are things. And beliefs are the content and substance of those thoughts. To really change your life, you don't have to change your thoughts. You have to change your beliefs.

Let's look at an extended example of how thoughts—and more importantly the beliefs that they encode—can have an impact not only on your approach to life but on the way your body helps or hinders you as you move through life. Suppose you have a job interview and you fully believe you are the right person for the job, although you don't have all the skills required. You don't let the fact that there are a few holes in your CV stop you from applying for the position, and you are confident in your abilities and not afraid to articulate them. You have upbeat emotions about this job and how you fit into it. Your positive attitude is fuelled by the belief that people tend to see the best in others, so you expect the interviewer will see the best in you. You are willing to learn new skills to fulfil all the job requirements and you believe that the interviewer will appreciate your ambition. Basically, you believe that the world is a good place, you are a competent person and challenges are really opportunities for growth.

As you arrive at the job interview these beliefs are already setting up a very real physical cascade of events: they stimulate positive, life-enhancing chemicals to flow through your brain and body, which then increases your mind–body coherence, which in turn helps you to up your performance level. The result is that you feel less stress than many people would experience in a job interview and you are able to naturally act more confidently and feel more relaxed. This relaxed body response helps you to think quickly and adeptly and to speak with clarity about your competence, knowledge, skills and experience. Almost everything that will occur in your job interview will have started with your belief about yourself, the world and other people.

Now let's explore the flip side of the situation. If you harbour conscious or subconscious self-limiting beliefs about your abilities or interview techniques, if you are running a tape loop of self-deflating inner talk ('I'm not intelligent enough', 'I'm not really qualified', 'I don't have enough experience') and if your overall belief system is one where the world is a hard place and others are only out for themselves so you always have to convince others of your worth and competence, then when it comes to interview time, your thoughts will be stimulating a surge of chemicals that put your body into a major stress response. Stress chemicals, such as adrenalin, when they are not overwhelming, can up your performance, making you sharp and focused. But when stress surges on the back of negative and fear-tinged beliefs, it reduces brain function, making you less articulate and dampening response time, so that you may stumble over answers or appear timid or confused. Stress chemicals affect memory, so that you may struggle to remember the questions you were going to ask or even the questions the interviewer just asked you. You may feel physically fidgety, anxious and nervous, and the interview will proceed accordingly.

Your thoughts control your biology. That's not an unsupported generalisation. Later in this book I will enlighten you with the current research from the frontiers of biology that show that our consciousness directly impacts cell function, in what Dr Bruce Lipton calls the 'biology of belief'.

The job interview examples I just laid out for you may appear self-evident—attitude affects behaviour. However, I hope by now you have been persuaded to consider that there is a lot more going on than emotion or attitude. The truth is that most of our beliefs are unconscious. They drive our behaviour and colour our life without our even knowing how or why.

Consider one other possibility in the job interview example: a person heads off to the job interview feeling well-qualified for the job and confident in presenting her qualifications. However, when she is actually on the spot in the interviewer's office, she suddenly wilts. She becomes a nervous wreck and doesn't even know why her confidence has crumbled and her eloquence—all those brilliant pre-planned answers and statements—has fled. Her attitude was confident and positive, but her unconscious self-limiting beliefs rose to the fore as she actually faced the interviewer. Beliefs do that—they rise up and expose the lie of our surface emotions.

We all know people who may not be very talented or qualified or whatever, but they are stellar at advocating for themselves and often win opportunities that we thought others might have better deserved. Are they just lucky or charmed? What do they have that so works to their advantage? The answer is not their positive attitude, but their underlying beliefs about themselves and the world. All those qualities we associate with a person's 'personality' are really the constellation of their core beliefs emerging as attitudes, emotions, actions, skills, gifts and so on. Add up all of the small and large, simplistic and complex, conscious and unconscious beliefs that you hold and that are driving your behaviour and personality at every moment of every day and you get a sense of how beliefs are said to create our reality, not just influence it.

I don't want to overdo my point, but let me present two more generalised, even simplistic examples of ways our unconscious beliefs can trip us up. Remember, the following are not attitudes, they are beliefs. Beliefs determine what your life will look like.

Example 1: Your goal is to improve your health, fitness and vitality, so you consider joining a gym, doing yoga or jogging. When you think of exercise, your immediate emotional reaction reveals the essence of your beliefs about the situation. Perhaps your immediate feelings include anxiety, boredom or even fear. These feelings could be driven by a set of beliefs that sound like the following inner self-talk:

❏ I've never been sporty or liked exercise.
❏ Exercise is hard work and draining.
❏ I'm too old for hard workouts.
❏ I don't have the time to exercise—just thinking about adding one more thing to my day drains me.

These beliefs belie a likely answer—you won't be exercising anytime soon. Or, if you do join the gym in that initial burst of surface enthusiasm, soon your core beliefs will have you finding reasons why perhaps the sofa and TV remote control may seem a better option.

How might the situation be different if the following were your true, spontaneous, unmediated inner self-talk?

❏ Exercise increases my vitality and energy, and I love to feel good.
❏ Health is important to me, and exercising is a major part of my wellness programme.
❏ Exercising keeps my body strong and flexible.

❏ A healthy body is a healthy mind.
❏ Exercise is a great way to relieve stress.

If you think you will never, ever think these thoughts, think again! There are ways to change your core beliefs from negative, self-defeating ones to positive, self-motivating ones. You can jump ahead in this book and get right to the exercises, but I suggest you slow down and take the time to read all the preliminary material so that you truly understand yourself and your belief patterns.

Example 2: Many of us are seeking a new romantic relationship and we all run an inner program about what we want that to look like, what we deserve and what we are likely to achieve. Which of the following set of core beliefs is the one likely to increase your chances of finding that new love?

❏ I am worthy of the best that love and romance has to offer.
❏ I experience joy, appreciation and fun in my romantic relationships.
❏ I am ready, willing and able for a passionate and exciting intimate relationship.
or
❏ Men/women cannot be trusted, I always end up getting hurt.
❏ Relationships are hard work and always seem to fail in the end.
❏ My chances of meeting anyone compatible with me are next to nil.

The fact is that if you have ever had a goal or desire in any area of your life and have fallen short of achieving it or given up on it, then barring a trauma or illness, you can almost always find that the fundamental reason for this lack of success is a set of self-limiting beliefs. The key point to take from this chapter is that our beliefs and perceptions precede and drive emotions, thoughts and behaviours. Everything we do is based on what we believe.

Here's a bizarre question for you: Where is your world? Let's go to Chapter 2 to find out... But first, the key points of this chapter.

Key Points

- ❏ Beliefs govern your feelings, thoughts and actions and influence every aspect of your life.
- ❏ Beliefs are very real electro-chemical signals that broadcast throughout your whole body.
- ❏ Your beliefs control your biology.
- ❏ Most of your beliefs are unconscious to you.

2

WHERE IS YOUR WORLD?

Our perceptions of what we see, hear, feel and so on depend to a great extent on our expectation. In a certain sense, what we perceive is what we expect.

Dr Stephen LaBerge

As we go through our day-to-day activities, our senses are bombarded with billions of 'bits' of information every minute. Our brain and nervous system are designed to filter huge amounts of this information from our conscious awareness so that we are not overloaded and can order the world, making sense of it. One way we order the inflow of information is through a filtering process, where we make deletions, form generalisations and sometimes create distortions. Most of the information that bypasses our conscious mind is either lost to us or is stored in our subconscious mind. It's for this reason that many scientists, especially psychologists and consciousness researchers, say that our subconscious mind is our primary mind and that most of who we are and how we act is influenced by the content of it.

How does this filtering process work? It's a complex process that I will talk about in greater depth again later, but for now we can keep the discussion relatively direct and simple. Think of a time when you were looking for a book on a crowded bookshelf. You couldn't find the title you were looking for. You checked again, and then again—but still no book. So you walked away or checked another bookcase elsewhere. Later you came back to the first bookcase, and lo and behold the book you were looking for popped out at you. It was there all along. You just couldn't see it. Your mind deleted it from your awareness. There are many reasons why this might have happened, from you being distracted thinking about something else to just being lazy and giving the bookshelf a cursory glance a couple of times. This kind of filtering happens all the time.

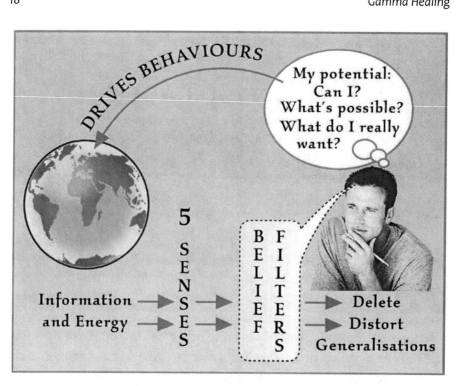

Figure 2 *Our beliefs act as our filters of perception. We perceive the information in our world through our five physical senses and make meaning of it based on what we believe to be true. Thus, in a fundamental way, the world really is as we believe it to be.*

I paid the price for it recently myself. I had new business cards printed with a different logo design that I was pleased with. I was so focused on the logo that I did not see that two of my phone numbers were scrambled. In fact, although I admired the new cards many times over the next few months, I never detected the incorrect phone numbers until I ran into someone I had given a card to and he told me he had been trying to call me but the numbers on my card didn't work. Arrgghhh!

Our daily lives are subject to the same kind of filtering processes. We screen our experiences according to our beliefs, focusing on what our beliefs tell us is important and ignoring or glossing over the rest. It's a stereotype, even a cliché, that women are bad drivers. Yet if you believed that were true, you would see many more erratic woman drivers than I would. According to your expectation of seeing them, you would see more mostly because you would be less tolerant of how women drive and, more importantly, because you would have a tendency to screen out seeing all of the skilled women drivers. We tend to filter the world for information that supports our belief system; conversely, we filter out that which contradicts it.

This truth answers the question that heads this chapter: where is your world? It's in our mind, in our subconscious and conscious belief systems. The world shows itself to us largely as we perceive it to be, so your world is a very different world from mine, according to our belief-filtering systems. When I explain more about how our minds work, in the next chapter, you will discover just how much information we delete from our conscious awareness. It truly boggles the mind!

Our beliefs and expectations can even edit our memories and revise reality. Elizabeth Loftus, Professor of Psychology at the University of California–Irvine, has conducted hundreds of experiments that have clearly shown that this revision process is real and how it works. In one study, adults who had visited the American theme park Disneyland, where actors are dressed as popular cartoon characters and wander the park interacting with visitors, were asked if they had talked to or otherwise interacted with Bugs Bunny while there. More than one third of them said they had. Several reported that they had shaken his hand or had even hugged him. Others remembered touching his tail or ear. Some even said they heard him say his famous line, 'What's up, Doc?' The problem is, Bugs Bunny is a Warner Brothers cartoon character, not a Walt Disney character. There is no Bugs Bunny character anywhere in the Disneyland theme park. But because there are other popular cartoon characters there, and because Bugs Bunny is among the most well known and well loved of cartoon characters, these adults expected he would be there, and thus many of them remembered seeing him, talking to him and even touching him. Their belief distorted the facts.

Our beliefs have many biases which can easily distort reality. Expectation is a major one, but so is the influence of authority. In his book *Influence*, social psychologist Dr Robert Cialdini showed that we tend to believe what is told to us by people whom we deem respected and trustworthy authority figures, such as physicians, scientists or people who are experts in their fields. We take their word at face value and tend not to check the facts they give us.

Dr Andrew Newberg, of the University of Pennsylvania, identified 27 ways in which we distort our reality to fit our biases. I have highlighted some of the primary ways below:

- ❏ **Family bias**—we tend to believe information given to us by family and close friends without too much question or checking of the facts. We have relied on these people, and we like and trust them, so we tend to believe them.
- ❏ **Attraction bias**—we tend to believe people whom we find attractive and who make eye contact with us more than we do those we deem unattractive or who tend not to look us in the eye. The reasons have to do with the positive emotions that arise in us when we view things or people we find aesthetically pleasing and when we receive another's attention.
- ❏ **Self-serving bias**—we tend to maintain those personal beliefs that benefit our own goals or interests.
- ❏ **Group consensus bias**—we tend to put more value on those beliefs that are shared by others; the more others agree with us, the truer our beliefs seem to be, even if they are not factually true. Conversely, the more people who disagree with our beliefs, the more we will begin to doubt these beliefs, even if they are true.
- ❏ **Projection bias**—we assume that people in the same group (religious, socio-economic etc.) as us have the same beliefs and view the world in a similar way. It's the 'everybody thinks like us' mindset.
- ❏ **Persuasion bias**—we tend to believe people more if they explain their view in a more emotional and concrete (visually stimulating, metaphorical, graphical) way. This bias can be positive or negative; consider the differing belief outcome of the persuasiveness of such powerful speakers as Martin Luther King, Jr. and Adolf Hitler.
- ❏ **Uncertainty bias**—generally, we do not deal well with feelings of uncertainty or ambiguity, so we prefer to hang on to some

beliefs, quickly form an opinion or make up our minds, or conversely to disbelieve facts about which we are unsure, rather than to remain uncertain for very long. We tend to do this even if it is to our advantage not to come to a conclusion or to wait to make a decision or form an opinion until we have more information.

❏ **Publication bias**—we tend to believe information that is published or reported in the media, such as on television or by some other seemingly reliable source, without asking too many questions. As an example, in 1976 the BBC broadcast that the planet Pluto would have a bizarre gravitational effect on Jupiter as it passed that planet, and the effect could be felt even on Earth. It reported that if you jumped at just the right time, you would experience a wonderful floating effect. Hundreds of people called in to say they had experienced it! Of course, no such effect was possible.

If you think you are immune to these kinds of belief biases and filters, think again. We all operate every day according to one or more of them. That's because we can't not have biases and filters. In some respects, we need them to survive, to avoid being inundated and overloaded with information, and to make sense of the information that does come our way. We don't have the time or the expertise to check every fact, consider every point of view or weigh up the ramifications of every option. We need to take action in order to live our lives; filtering information is one way we do that. However, we can all benefit from exploring which of our belief filters help or hinder our innate abilities, goals, dreams and desires. To live the life we really want, we have to ask which of our filters is beneficial to us or not, empowering to us or not, life-enhancing or not.

We have not only personal filters, but mass ones as well. These are formed from our cultural, religious, economic, political and other influences. As a quick check of your more generalised belief filters, complete each of the following sentences with the first words that come to mind. Do not edit yourself!

❏ Most politicians are...
❏ Most Americans are...
❏ Most Muslims are...
❏ Most Italians are...
❏ Most Catholics are...
❏ Most doctors are...
❏ Most lawyers are...

If you are like most people, your unedited, spontaneous statements were probably generalised statements, perhaps bordering on stereotypes. That's because we are very good at making huge generalisations based on our beliefs. We tend to generalise about what is true or false, right or wrong, possible or not possible and so on based on our past experiences, on what we have been taught, and on news and information to which we have been exposed repeatedly. These mass generalisations often become prejudices. The truth is that we don't often stop to question our assumptions and prejudices, never mind our core constellation of beliefs. Yet doing so can be one of the most liberating activities of our lives, because we inevitably discover that we didn't even decide according to our own logic or intellect, or even our own free will, to hold most of our beliefs. We were programmed to hold them!

The way we form beliefs involves a host of influences that are working on us from the moment of our birth. As children we depend on others to teach us about the way the world is. We learn a specific language, which in and of itself structures what we are even capable of conceiving and believing. For example, some languages have no words with which to talk about the future, focusing only on the past or the present. Imagine how different such a world is from your own! You also may have been raised with a particular religion or family politics, or with a specific family attitude about the value of science, art, logic and creativity. You were brought up to expect a certain type of emotional expressiveness, perhaps in a family that did not hug or touch much, which coloured the way you view relationships, intimacy and so on. The fact is that we are exposed to myriad ways, both blatant and subtle, to filter the world.

You were taught what to include and ignore, what to value and devalue, and so on and so on.

For most of us, our early years are ones in which we didn't think for ourselves at all or very much; we simply accepted what we were told and formed beliefs based on what those around us believed. That's all well and good. Children, after all, have to learn some way and from someone. But as adults, we find that running the same belief programme we had as children no longer serves us well. So, it pays to become conscious of all the ways we form our beliefs in the first place. The majority of our beliefs came from:

❑ Parents/family
❑ Media
❑ Social/economic class
❑ Geographical location
❑ Culture
❑ Religion
❑ History
❑ Science
❑ Schools
❑ Friends/colleagues/peers
❑ Political system

The truth is that, as Albert Einstein once said, 'common sense is the collection of prejudices acquired by the age of eighteen'.[1] And that is the problem: we take all those beliefs—many of which are prejudices—into our adulthood unquestioned and uninvestigated. We inherit so many of our beliefs at such a deeply subconscious level that they still control our choices and actions today, even when the choices and actions of yesterday are making our todays miserable.

I am suggesting that the way out of this dilemma, and the way to finally gain conscious control over your life to remake it to meet your loftiest goals, is to increase your awareness of what your core beliefs are and then to transform those that are not serving you into ones that are. It is possible to do so, without years of 'talk therapy' or involved self-analysis. Logic holds no sway over the subconscious, which is why all our good intentions and New Year resolutions so often fail. The door to the unconscious is through the body, as I will soon show you. There are quick and effective ways to create an internal life that dynamically supports the way you want your external life to look. You can begin the process by reflecting on the following three questions now:

1. What beliefs and ways of being have you inherited from your parents and childhood upbringing?
2. What areas of your life are not the way you would like them to be?
3. What behaviours do you adopt in those areas and what must your beliefs be that drive those behaviours?

As a simple example, I had a coaching client who was always raising issues at home and at work. She would always bring an issue up in a meeting and she was not sure why she did this. At first she assumed that there must be a part of her that liked conflict, but that didn't feel right to her. After just a small bit of enquiry she realised she was playing out quite unconsciously a belief from her parents that was 'never sleep on an argument'. Her parents, quite literally, wanted closure on any disagreement or heated discussion before they went to bed and she was playing a version of this in her own mind.

Another simple example from my own life comes from a belief that I inherited from my mother. As a child she believed that milk was a 'meal in a drink' and it was the best thing for you. From a young boy to the age of about 16, every day I would drink three or four pints of full-fat, pasteurised milk! It wasn't until I started studying nutrition and updating my own belief systems that I realised that perhaps this was not the healthiest option. My mother comes from a farming family and was born on a farm back in the 1930s. Her father milked cows every day so it is quite easy to see where her belief came from.

Just take a few minutes to reflect on the three questions above and see if you can highlight any limiting outdated beliefs you may have inherited.

* * *

Almost all of our beliefs are ones we hold from the past, so it is no surprise that many of them are out of date and need revising. It is important to keep some perspective here. Note the words I used: 'beliefs are out of date'. They are not necessarily good or bad. They are just old. They no longer work in your present reality. The change is not to replace a bad belief with a good one. It's to replace an outdated one with an updated one. You have changed, the world has changed and your circumstances in the world have changed from when you were a child. What you wanted as a child may no longer be what you choose as an adult. If your life is not working as you would like it to, it's no surprise if you are operating on a constellation of outdated beliefs. Your beliefs filter your world, and thus they control your potential.

So isn't it time you aligned your beliefs about the world with the world you actually live in now? Doing so is the key to changing your life, the key to making conscious choices that foster all the abundance, health, happiness, love and creativity that you desire now and in the future. In a very real sense, as paradoxical as it sounds, you are what you believe you are capable of being!

Physicist and author Dr Jeremy Hayward sums things nicely when he tells us:

> To a very large extent men and women are a product of how they define themselves. As a result of a combination of innate ideas and the intimate influence of the culture and the environment we grow up in, we come to have beliefs about the nature of being human.
>
> These beliefs penetrate to a very deep level of our psychosomatic systems, our minds and brains, our nervous systems, our endocrine systems, and even our blood and sinews. We act, speak, and think according to these deeply held beliefs and beliefs systems.[2]

I can pretty much guarantee, based on my experience as a psychologist in change performance and after working with thousands of

people, that you have out-of-date self-limiting beliefs that are holding you back from realising the fullness of your personal potential
and abilities in all aspects of your life: self-esteem, relationships,
finances, prosperity, work and career, health and fitness, sports performance and self-healing abilities.

And I can tell you that changing these outdated beliefs is not
difficult. However, information is power, so before we work on
changing your beliefs, it's helpful to have a better understanding of
how and where these beliefs live within you—in your mind. But
what exactly is the mind? Let's find out...

Key Points

- ❏ We filter the world for information that supports our belief
  systems.
- ❏ We inherited most of our beliefs from our parents and our
  environment.
- ❏ Almost all of our beliefs are based on our past experiences and
  so by definition are out of date.
- ❏ The most powerful way to create lasting change in your life is to
  change and update your beliefs.

3

WHAT EXACTLY IS THE MIND?

*The mind, once expanded to the dimensions of larger ideas,
never returns to its original size.*

Oliver Wendell Holmes

Of all the wonders of the world, among the most wondrous is the human mind. The power of the mind is awe inspiring and we tend to think of its seemingly extraordinary capacities as miraculous. We have all heard stories about the nearly unbelievable powers of the mind: orchestrating spontaneous remissions of disease through mind–body interactions, directing the body to display Herculean feats of strength in emergencies, marshalling astonishing powers of will and perseverance during extreme hardships, erupting in insights and epiphanies that pop up out of the blue and birthing the new and the novel through displays of creativity and inventiveness. It's no surprise, then, that in those quiet moments when we ponder the meaning of life and of our place in it, other than thinking perhaps how nice chocolate tastes and how stunning the sunset is, our ponderings often lead us to those deeper questions like: *What is the mind and how powerful is it?*

Answering these questions has been the province of philosophers and sages throughout history, and in modern times of scientists too. It is still orthodox scientific belief that the mind, and consciousness itself, is an emergent property of the 'wet matter' of the brain, a by-product of its electro-chemical activity. Let us be clear that this is a belief and not a scientific fact. In this chapter and others, we will explore why. And in doing so, we will delve into the newest, most provocative and exciting research and insights that help us understand not only what our mind is but also how we can use the power of our mind to transform ourselves and our lives.

We begin by jumping headlong into the scientific debate. Going back 100 years to the early 1900s, British biologist Sir Julian

Huxley asked the question, 'Is the brain a good enough explanation for describing the mind?' His answer was emphatic: 'The brain alone is not responsible for the mind, even though it is a necessary organ for its manifestation.'[1] In more recent times visionary biologist Dr Rupert Sheldrake explained:

> *The theory that the mind is in the brain is a dogma based on the authority of science, and most people never think of questioning it. Few are even aware that it is a theory at all, and accept it as a scientific truth.*[2]

While there is no question that the brain is crucial to the proper functioning of some aspects of the mind (since brain injury and disease can affect memory, logic, reasoning and more), other frontier scientists are telling us that the mind is not entirely dependent on the brain. It seems to extend beyond the brain and even outside of the body: there is even very well-validated evidence of the reality of a collective and global mind! Frontier science is revealing the extent to which the mind must be thought of as an energy and information field that interpenetrates every cell of the body and spreads out beyond the body to connect to the entire cosmos and everything in it. We'll look at this inspiring research in later chapters. For now, let's venture only a short way beyond the boundaries of accepted belief.

The Mind–Body Connection

So what if the brain—and by extension, therefore, the mind—was not only in the skull? Dr Candace Pert has spent her career changing the paradigm of biology, especially as it relates to brain chemicals. She has shown how our brains manufacture certain biochemicals when we think and feel. Technically, some of these biochemicals are called neuropeptides, but she has labelled them the 'molecules of emotion'.[3] These neuropeptides are the messenger molecules of the brain—the way our thoughts transfer themselves into molecules that then affect our entire body. For example, if you are feeling anxiety, your body makes its own valium in just the right quantity to help calm you. If you feel exhilarated, your brain and body produce more of a molecule called interleukin 2, but when you feel overly stressed, your levels of interleukin 2 go down. Why does that matter? Because interleukin 2 has been discovered to be a powerful immune system booster and it shows promise as an anti-cancer drug. Stress reduces its levels, compromising your immune system. Now there's a good reason to get exhilarated regularly!

Dr Pert's work and that of many others has demonstrated clearly that your mood affects your immune system directly, at the molecular level. Every thought and emotion has a biochemical equivalent. We literally have chemicals for love, anger, happiness, guilt, lust and so on.

These 'molecules of emotion' were once thought to be manufactured only by the brain and nervous system. However, Dr Pert's research revealed they are made by many other systems in the body and they can affect every cell in the body, not just the cells of the nervous system.[4] The mind, then, is in a very literal sense a whole-body phenomenon. One of Dr Pert's conclusions is that the body actually is the subconscious mind. Instead of the brain being the commander and chief of the body, her work reveals that mind—our beliefs and perceptions, thoughts and emotions—commands the brain and the body to produce the correlated molecules. It is the mind, working through the brain, that organises and coordinates all the metabolic functions necessary for life and survival. To use a musical metaphor, we now have to think of the brain as the piano and the mind as the pianist playing the music throughout the body.

This is a radically different picture of the mind–brain hierarchy than most of us learned in school. Unless you have read the literature outside of the now outdated biology and medicine, and outside of the mainstream press, you won't have realised that over the last few decades, as physician Daniel Monti has said,

> *The evidence has mounted persuasively that the mind and body are inextricably connected, with our thoughts affecting our*

biology in ways never before thought possible. We truly are fully integrated beings.[5]

From the evidence amassed by frontier biologists, it is now possible to say that we truly cannot know where the mind stops and the body begins, and vice versa.

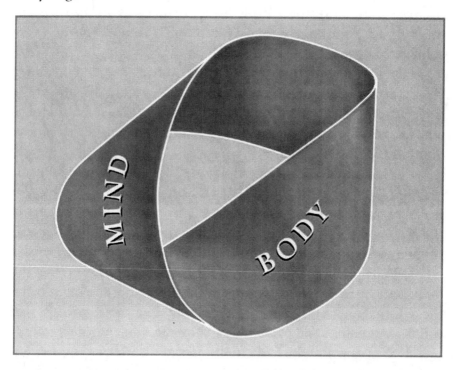

Figure 3.1   *The mind and body are fully integrated systems, not separate ones. Imagine a ribbon where on one side you write the word 'body' and on the other the word 'mind'. If you twist the ribbon once and then connect the two ends together, it forms a Mobius strip. If you now trace along the ribbon from the word 'body' on what appears to be the inside of the ribbon, you will see how you end up on the word 'mind' on what seems to be the outside of the ribbon, yet you have crossed no defined boundary between inside and outside.*

The Dual Mind

Psychologists identify two separate minds: the conscious mind and the subconscious mind. I've talked a bit about them already, and it's time now to dive into this fascinating reality in more detail.

Your conscious mind is the thinking part that is associated with your personal identity. It is involved in logic, reasoning and decision making, although it is also the seat of much of your creativity and from which you direct your free will. It is associated with your 'ego', a term described in various ways by different schools of psychology, but that you can generally understand as the 'you' you think you are and that you show the world on a consistent basis, day to day.

Your 'other' mind is the subconscious, which also is described variously by different schools of psychology, but is generally known to be the place of your programmed and learned actions, responses and behaviours. All of the involuntary systems of the body are run by the subconscious mind, which is pretty impressive. For example, your heart beats approximately 100,000 times a day, sending over 100 gallons of blood through your vascular system, yet you don't have to consciously tell it to do so or direct its action. Likewise, it is below the level of conscious awareness—hence, it is subconscious—that each of your 60 trillion or more cells performs staggering numbers of functions every second. Enzymes are secreted in the exact amounts required in order to digest food. Blood is filtered at the precise rate by the kidneys to make urine and excrete waste. You get the idea—every one of the millions, perhaps trillions, of other functions and processes that keep you alive and active are harmoniously balanced by your subconscious mind.

Your subconscious functioning is absolutely crucial to your life. And yet, as you are about to discover, the majority of your mental and emotional reactions are also processed at a subconscious level. This may be limiting the quality of your life and the amount of potential you are expressing.

Let's look at the big picture again. From midway through our gestation as a foetus into childhood and beyond, our life experiences are recorded and stored in the subconscious mind. As a foetus we not only receive nutrients from our mother but also 'molecules of emotion' from our mother's reactions to her environment. It is suggested that 52% of our intelligence is determined by the environment while in utero.[6] These early experiences

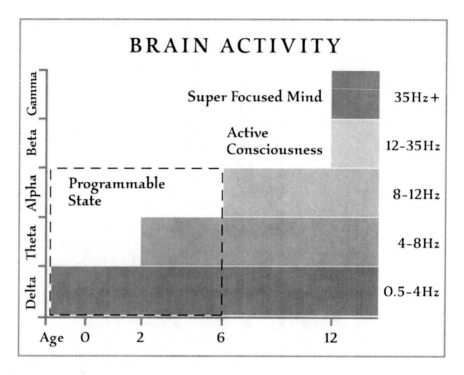

Figure 3.2   *There is a correlation between brainwave activity and how we download the 'rules of life' during our first six years. Image reproduced with kind permission of Dr Bruce Lipton.*

and the influx of new information we experience throughout childhood combine to create our beliefs, which determine the 'rules' that shape the way we create everything in our lives, from our personal relationships to our profession, and our decisions about our future.

Figure 3.2 illustrates just how much of our subconscious is open to 'programming', to use a computer metaphor, by outside influences, such as our parents, teachers, culture and more.[7] The process is quite fascinating, as it appears to be aligned with brain wave activity. Generally, we have five levels of brain-wave activity: gamma, alpha, beta, theta and delta. The gamma brain waves are not often activated in our daily life but when they are they create a super-focused mind state. The alpha wave correlates to a relaxed, calm state of consciousness, a state in which we often experience heightened levels of intuition and creativity. When the brain is in the alpha state, the body is usually relaxed and the two hemispheres of the brain are more coherent. This creates increased whole-brain functioning that is often associated with high performance states and a balance between intelligence and logic and wisdom and insight.

Beta brain waves kick in when we actively think and direct our attention, as in problem solving or in dealing with external stimuli. A quick switch to a beta-wave state often signals the rise of panic or the flight-or-fight feeling. Theta waves are associated with states of deep meditation, trance and light sleep. Delta waves arise mostly during deep sleep. The Gamma Belief Change Technique and Gamma Brain Technique© create large amounts of gamma, theta and alpha brain waves (see page 169).

For the first two years of life, we are predominantly in a delta brainwave pattern. Although this is deep sleep for adults, infants and very young children produce delta waves when they are conscious. They are downloading massive amounts of environmental and emotional data, so a king up the world through their five senses and recording and storing it in their subconscious mind for later use.

From about the ages of 2 to 6 years, our brain switches to a predominantly theta brain-wave state, which represents dreaminess and contemplation. This is when many children develop imaginary worlds, as they mix up their external and interior worlds.

After about age 6, we exist mostly in the alpha brain wave range, until we reach about age 12, when beta waves predominate. These states coincide with the start of school, where logic and reason become our primary mode of learning and of processing information.

From midway through pregnancy and the first six years of life, a child is in a highly programmable brain-wave state, one often referred to as the hypnagogic state. This has been found to be a 'super learning' state. It is why young children can absorb huge amounts of information and can be taught so easily. For example, they can almost effortlessly become fluent in several languages at the same time if they are exposed to them on a daily basis. In these formative years, a child does not have to be specifically shown and coached by his or her parents to learn behaviours; information is learned and behaviours adopted simply by exposure and observation. This early programming also includes downloading the core information and opinions that form the essence of our feelings of self worth and of our perceived gifts and abilities. During this time we lay down the foundation of our social self and the fundamental style of our social and interpersonal interactions.

So, whereas consciously you may feel and think that you are in charge of the quality, condition and direction of your life, the truth is that at a subconscious level you may be simply living out patterns and programs that you learned from others during your childhood and that now in your adulthood may be taking you in the opposite direction from or causing conflict against achieving your desires and goals.

Your subconscious software is like the software that runs on your computer. You may have loaded many software programs when you first got your computer, and now, many years later, you may be using only a few of them. However, the unused programs are still there, running in the background, using electricity, energy and resources. Your subconscious beliefs do the same—they run without you being aware of them, often depleting your inner resources, putting stress on your nervous system and upsetting your mind–body coherence and subtly leading you in a way that is not in line with your conscious goals. This is why it is essential that as an adult you become aware of your subconscious programs, update them and align them with your conscious goals and desires. When you do, you have a much greater chance of creating the type of life you desire because your subconscious mind holds an enormous amount of power. It is power you have at your disposal, to use to your benefit. Let's now explore just how much power you have stored inside you, awaiting your conscious attention and action.

The Power of Your Subconscious Mind

The conscious and subconscious minds can be likened to information processors, each being able to process a certain amount of energy and information. Think of each as having a certain bandwidth of processing power that can be measured in bits per second (bps). As a comparison with our mind, a telephone can transmit and receive information at a bandwidth of 4000 bps and a modern radio receiver at 16,000 bps.[8] Staggeringly, the processing power of the subconscious mind is a whopping 40,000,000 bits of information per second! Now compare that with the conscious mind, which can process a mere 40 bits of information per second. The subconscious mind has one million times more processing power than the conscious mind.[9] As a visual metaphor to help you get your head around the differences in processing power of the two minds, take a look at Figure 3.3, which shows the British Houses of Parliament and the famous clock tower Big Ben. Imagine that every pixel in the image is a bit of data converted into nerve impulses then information inside your brain. Let's say that the image has 40 million pixels or bits of data. Your subconscious mind would download and process enough information every second to

Figure 3.3 *This image contains at least 40 million 'bits', each called a pixel. There are approximately 40 million neural impulses taking place in your brain every second. Of these 40 million, you become conscious of only about 40 of these bits of information, which then make up your reality. The rest are processed at the subconscious level. There is a lot more going on inside of you than you are aware of!*

equal all the pixels that make up this image. In one second—boom your subconscious would download the whole image. Now what you would become conscious of is a different matter entirely. In the same second, that amount of information that would bubble up to your conscious awareness is shown in Figure 3.4. Not much, is it?

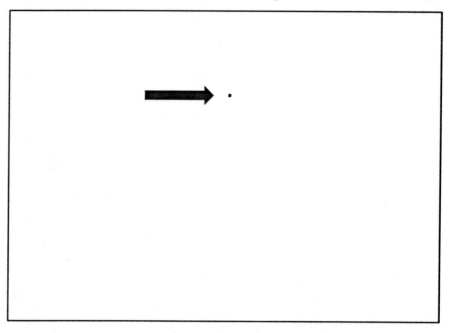

Figure 3.4   *Your conscious mind is extremely limited in its processing capacity, which is about one million times less than the processing capacity of your subconscious mind.*

Remember back in Chapter 2 where I talked about how we all delete massive amounts of the information that is available to us and how we choose to slant, ignore or otherwise revise much of the information that we do take in? Now you can appreciate just how much of the world is being processed inside you that you are not aware of consciously. And you can also appreciate why it is important to access your subconscious to become aware of how the massive amounts of information you are storing there will be influencing your beliefs, actions and intentions, controlling the quality of your life.

Now here's the real kicker: What percentage of your day-to-day thoughts, feelings and actions is coming from your conscious choices, as compared to those that are learned programs and behaviours coming from your subconscious mind?

Astonishingly, 95–99% of all your thoughts, feelings and actions each day is governed by learned programs in your subconscious mind.[10] Almost everything that you think and do in life is driven from a level of mind you are not aware of! No doubt, you have experienced this truth in diverse ways. For instance, if you've ever had a 'Freudian slip' you know what I am talking about. A Freudian slip is usually an embarrassing slip of the tongue, when you say something other than what you intended, without even realising it until it is too late. These slips of the tongue arise from our subconscious mind, usually when we feel one way but won't speak that truth, deliberately hiding our true feelings. Our subconscious 'outs' us and our true feelings. As an example, imagine a woman who has a crush on a guy she sees around town a lot but has never met. She knows his name and thinks he's the handsomest man on earth, but she's too shy to introduce herself. One day, while talking to a friend, this friend mentions the man's name. The woman blurts out, 'You know hunk?' instead of 'You know him?'.

Another example of our subconscious programming at work is that once we learn how to do something well, we don't have to work consciously to carry out that action. If you drive, you've probably experienced arriving at your destination and realising you were not very aware of having made the journey. Having learned and 'downloaded' the driving program, you only have to have the intent and the program plays without any conscious awareness required. Riding a bike, getting dressed, cooking a favourite meal—many of the activities that fill our lives have become rote-learned subconscious programs.

Many of these subconscious and rote programs are essential, as we cannot think consciously about more than a couple of things at the same time. In an ideal world, everyone would be aware of all their behaviours, actions, and thoughts; however, in the fast-paced modern world, this is simply an impossibility—and it may always have been so, since we are capable of processing so much information that we don't need on a moment-to-moment basis. We have to screen out some of these streams of information so as not to be overwhelmed. However, the downside of our lack of awareness is that although the conscious mind can be incredibly creative, it can also be incredibly demanding and busy. It flits from one thought to another very quickly, and that can be a recipe for inefficiency, diversion and the many excuses that keep us from living up to our potential and realising our goals. In addition, most of us grow comfortable with the people we see on a regular basis and our interactions become rote. As their behaviours and emotional responses become familiar and predictable, so do ours. This can make for a comfortable existence without too many surprises to 'upset the applecart' of our lives. But it can also mean that our marriage, friendships, work relations and other kinds of relationships suffer from neglect and boredom.

You might be surprised at just how unruly your conscious mind is and how rote you have become in your interactions with others. As a test, pay attention over the next few hours—and if you can remember to, over the next few days—to the thoughts that flit through your mind. You might just be appalled at how easily distracted your conscious mind gets and how often you are acting from rote programming, almost robotically. You may also find that if you start to observe your inner voice you will realise it never stops. It is constantly on the go, talking about past experiences or future events.

There are many kinds of awareness techniques you can practise to return to 'in-the-moment consciousness'—to aim to stop playing back these potentially limiting rote behaviours and responses. Try a few of these and see how they work for you. They can provide clues to how you are thinking, feeling and acting at a subconscious level.

Can you become more conscious?

1. Stop what you are doing and count how many comfortable slow deep belly breaths you take in one minute. Keep your mind totally focused on your breathing. See if you can keep totally present for the minute. Let's say you do eight breaths in the minute, you can now use that as a benchmark. Throughout the day, aim to do a minimum of three sets of eight slow deep belly breaths. You know that you will have completed about a minute of conscious 'in-the-moment' living each time. This will relax and balance your brain, mind and body.

2. For just one minute a day, attempt to remain totally conscious of the present moment. Observe your thoughts and feelings without judgement, while remaining present in your body and grounded in the here and now. When you can stay totally focused and mindful of the present moment and all that is going on in you during that moment, then increase your observation time, seeing how long you can stay conscious of your thoughts, feelings and actions. Observe what happens with no judgement, just let it be, your goal is simply to observe.

3. Carry out the same awareness exercise while you are in conversation with someone, intending to be truly present to that person and listen to what he or she is saying. There are generally two types of listening. The first type is to listen with the intent to reply, which naturally is what most of us do. We have already formulated our answers or the next part of the conversation before we have truly listened to the other person. The second type of listening is listening with the intent to truly understand the other person's point of view and situation. So in your next conversation, really intend to listen and understand the person before you reply. Easy as it sounds, you may find it takes some practice.

4. Do the one-minute mindfulness/conscious awareness exercise while you are in a busy environment, such as walking down a busy street or while shopping. When you focus your awareness and really pay attention, you will discover just how much information is coming at you every moment of every day. You are taking most of it in, only now you are increasing what you are taking in consciously instead of mostly subconsciously.

5. Go somewhere you can 'people watch' with the sole aim of doing it without judgement. Simply observe what people are doing and what your inner thoughts and feelings are about what you witness. When you observe your thoughts and feelings and listen to your inner dialogue about it, you will begin to learn what beliefs you have that are driving those thoughts. You can then decide whether they are empowering beliefs or limiting beliefs that need to be upgraded.

Being more conscious on a daily basis and making time for self-reflection and quieting the mind are potentially life-transforming practices.

By now hopefully it is clear that when your conscious mind is busy thinking about past experiences or future intentions and desires, your subconscious is also at work, driving the behaviours that you show to the world. These behaviours may seem like you are consciously choosing them, but actually that is an illusion as they are driven from the subconscious. It is your subconscious that is dictating the 'story' of your life to you.

It is very important to understand, however, that the subconscious mind is fairly straightforward—it is mainly a stimulus and response system; what is programmed in is what comes out. Have you ever had an experience where someone 'pushed your buttons'? When someone said something to you that created an autopilot emotional reaction? It is not what that person said or did, especially if you just met him or her. It is how it was said, including the body language and facial expressions, that may have stirred subconscious memories within you, those past programs you are running automatically. It is from those subconscious memories that your actions and responses arise, and remember that a minimum of 95% of the time we are doing this. This blows my mind: in effect we are robots, prisoners of our personal and cultural beliefs and conditioning. There is no freedom here until we make the choice to break free from this and claim our mind back!

Imagine you are 7 years old, and you are looking for your favourite toy, say a teddy bear, but you can't find it. You go to your mum to ask her where it might be. She is in the kitchen preparing dinner, standing at the worktop chopping vegetables to make soup. You notice that she is in slippers and her hair is up in curlers. You ask her where your teddy bear is, and she replies that she thinks that you are now too old to play with a teddy bear and that she got rid of it. As the reality of what she has done sinks in, a massive surge of chemicals flows through your body as a mix of emotions erupts: disbelief, shock, pain, rage and more. The situation is highly charged emotionally and even though you may act up, yelling at your mum or even crying, most of the emotions and meaning of the moment get stored in your subconscious.

Now fast forward 15 years. You are going to dinner for the first time at the house of a girl you have recently begun dating. You make an error about what time you are supposed to arrive and get to her house early. She comes to the door and lets you in, saying she is not ready yet. As she leads you to the kitchen, you notice that she has her hair pinned up and is wearing slippers. When you get to the kitchen, she finishes adding spices to the vegetable soup she is cooking. There is some sliced bread on a board on the worktop. You really like her, but suddenly you feel a strong aversion to the situation, and even to her, but you have no idea why. Your uneasy feelings are inexplicable and you can't seem to shake them. What's more, they colour the whole evening and you start to question whether you fancy her as much as you thought you did. The date does not go so well. You drive home wondering why.

As you can now guess, the situation had close associations at the subconscious level to the previously stored highly charged event with your mum and the loss of your teddy bear, an event you may not even now remember or think you care about. But in your subconscious you both remember and care. Now this may seem a very simple and almost silly example, but I can assure you this type of thing is happening all the time. Unless we are 'Buddha-like' and totally living in the present moment, the majority of our reactions are based on past subconscious experiences.

We all have such occurrences in our lives. I'll share one of mine that is not too dissimilar to the one above. I was in a relationship with a girl I really liked, but frequently we had harsh autopilot reactions to one another. Our emotional buttons were always being pushed. After some open and honest communication and exploration between us, I realised that some of the ways she looked at or spoke to me triggered my subconscious memory of how my mother talked to me as a teenager. As you can probably guess, my relationship with this girl was not really only with this woman—it was at some deep level with my mum as well, which is not good for a romantic relationship! As my girlfriend reflected on how she reacted to me, she became aware of how I mirrored some behaviours she associated with her father. Our relationship entered a whole new level of appreciation, enjoyment and passion when we came to these realisations and updated our old subconscious programs with new ones.

If our subconscious is what is influencing our thoughts, emotions and behaviours a minimum of 95% of the time, this type of phenomenon is happening to us most of the time. We are feeling, thinking and behaving from outdated subconscious beliefs and programs, and there is not much creativity or freedom in doing that. These outdated programs are the most severe limits to our realising our potential and living the quality of lives we truly desire. So, let's continue with our exploration of how our minds work so we can get closer to learning how we can overcome these limits and free ourselves to our unlimited potential.

Key Points

- ❑ Your mind is in every cell of your body.
- ❑ The mind and body are one complete system.
- ❑ Your subconscious mind is one million times more powerful in processing information than your conscious mind.
- ❑ At least 95% of the day your thoughts, feelings and actions are based on learned programs stored in the subconscious mind.

4

HOW CONSCIOUS ARE YOU?

The mind is like an iceberg, it floats with one-seventh of its bulk under water.

Sigmund Freud

During one of my public workshops, I had just finished explaining the difference between the conscious and sub-conscious minds when a woman in the group offered a personal story. She related that she had spent a year in a Buddhist monastery, during which time she had learned to meditate. She had been told that we are less than 1% conscious and that after years of dedicated meditation we may get to a level where we use 10% of our conscious awareness. My comment about what she had shared was along the lines of that I appreciated how the Buddhists' view agreed with science. The woman quickly cor-rected me, saying, 'Don't you mean it is good that science has finally caught up with Buddhist knowledge and wisdom?' On reflection, I have to agree that she was quite right. Brain science is only about 100 years old compared to Buddhism's 1000 or more years of existence.

However, from the science I have already shared with you, you know that we don't have to rely on Buddhist wisdom to tell us that there is a glaring disparity between the way we use our subcon-scious versus conscious minds. In this chapter, I share with you more of the fascinating, and even startling research that shows how dependent we are on our subconscious mind in the running of our everyday life.

Benjamin Libet, Professor Emeritus of Physiology at the University of California, San Francisco, has devoted 30 years to researching the processes that occur in our conscious and sub-conscious minds. He came to one of his most fundamental dis-coveries through a rather simple experiment in which he asked research volunteers to move their wrists at a time of their own choosing while they also observed a graphic on a computer of a dot moving around a clock face. They were asked to note the exact time when they decided to move their wrist. It is important to note that they were to identify not when they moved their wrist, but when they first had the thought, 'I am going to move my wrist now.' They were hooked up to equipment that could detect their overall brain activity, so that a correlation could be made between when they thought about moving their wrist and the spike in brain-wave activity that corresponded with their making a decision and actually flexing their wrists. The data gathered from the experiment revealed that on average their brain became more active about 200 milliseconds before they actually flexed their wrist. This in and of itself is not so surprising a result, as it takes about 200 milliseconds for the signals from the brain to get to the wrist to instruct it to move. However, Libet was also monitoring the specific area of the participants' brains that was involved with controlling muscle movement, and this part of the brain showed a spike in activity 350 milliseconds *before* the participant became conscious of having made the decision to move his or her wrist.[1] He called this the 'readiness potential' (see Figure 4.1).

Other researchers were as startled by the results of this experiment as was Professor Libet. For example, Dr Gerald Zaltman, of Harvard Business School, said

> *This shows us that the areas of the human brain that involve choice are activated well before we become consciously aware that we have made a choice. That is, decisions happen before they are seemingly made.*[2]

What Dr Libet has shown, and what Dr Zaltman is saying, is that our subconscious self is actually 'in charge'. That blows my mind! How about you?

Dr Libet's research had focused on areas of the brain involved in movement. Later research looked at less concrete, and more amorphous, areas of brain activity. For example, in 2008 a team led

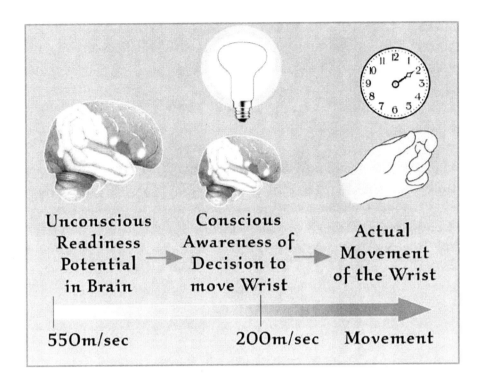

Unconscious   Conscious
Readiness   Awareness of   Actual
Potential   →   Decision to   →   Movement
in Brain   move Wrist   of the Wrist

550m/sec   200m/sec   Movement

Figure 4.1 *When you make a decision, your brain processes information milliseconds before you are actually consciously aware that you have made a decision. This means that in some very real way the decisions you make arise first from your subconscious mind.*

by Dr John-Dylan Haynes of the Bernstein Centre for Computational Neuroscience in Berlin, Germany, conducted a study to try to detect the same kind of readiness potential in the higher thought centres of the brain, such as the prefrontal cortex and parietal cortex, which are associated with abstract thought and decision making. In one of his experiments, volunteers held a device in each hand that had a push button on it. The volunteers were also hooked up to machines that could detect their brain activity in these specific brain areas. They were told simply to push one of the two buttons whenever they were ready. The result was that the volunteers' brains showed activity in these two centres 10 seconds before they actually pushed one of the buttons. That means their subconscious mind knew 10 seconds before their conscious minds did which button they had decided to push! The effect was so reliable that the researchers could predict with almost 100% certainty which button would be pushed before the volunteer actually made the decision to push one button rather than the other. Ten seconds is an eternity in terms of brain activity. Processes in the body happen in milliseconds, even nanoseconds. So the fact that there was this much of a delay between brain activity indicating a decision, and the volunteer feeling they were making the decision and immediately carrying it out, was an astounding finding.

Dr Patrick Haggard, of the Institute of Cognitive Neuroscience at University College London, concluded,

> *We all think that we have a conscious free will. However, this study shows that actions come from preconscious [another term for subconscious] brain activity patterns and not from the person consciously thinking about what they are going to do.*[3]

As Carl Jung expressed it many years ago, 'the conscious rises out of the unconscious like an island newly risen from the sea'.[4] The scientific truth is that, as Harvard professor of psychology Daniel Wegner said less poetically but more pointedly, 'It usually seems that we consciously will our voluntary actions, but this is an illusion.'[5]

The implication of this research is, of course, that in order to make the best conscious decisions, it is absolutely essential that we have our subconscious programs up to date and in alignment with our conscious desires. If we don't, we are treating our minds in ways we wouldn't even treat our computers. Would you run your computer on software that is decades old? Would you put up with the resulting limitations and inefficiencies? Would you be content to be unable to access the latest and greatest applications because the software won't recognise it or interface with it? I don't think anyone reading this book would. So, the question arises, why are you content to be running outdated, limiting and inefficient internal programs—the programs of your subconscious mind?

Let's revisit the data from Chapter 3: your subconscious mind is a 40-million-bit processor that operates at least 95% of the time, whereas your conscious mind is a 40-bit processor that operates only about 5% of the time. When you update and reprogram your subconscious mind to be in alignment with your conscious goals, you utilise this vast processing power to efficiently make connections between your subconscious and conscious mind. Once the link is established, you bring all of your resources, not just some of them, to bear on making your desires a reality and attaining your loftiest goals. To use another analogy, think of a pilot flying an airliner from London to New York. The pilot can expend enormous energy doing everything himself—such as managing trajectory, altitude, velocity and such like—or he can program the plane's autopilot with the destination data and let the plane fly itself. Being able to trust your subconscious as your autopilot can free you in ways you can barely now imagine.

Furthermore, reprogramming your subconscious with new belief programs sets up resonant energy through your mind and body that extends out into the environment, attracting towards you the necessary elements to accomplish your desired goals more easily and quickly. I know that statement may seem overly metaphysical and, for some readers, even downright unbelievable, but later I will be presenting evidence of how we project our personal energy signature into the environment 24 hours a day. When your energy is coherent everything in life seems to go more smoothly and be more enjoyable, with less resistance and challenge.

Carl Jung theorised about the 'meaningful coincidences' in life—which he studied seriously as they occurred with his patients and in his own life—that make it seem as if the universe has heard our inner voice and is responding to our unspoken needs and wishes. These synchronicities take many forms, from running into an old friend you haven't seen for decades but happened to be thinking of, to needing the solution to a problem and opening a newspaper to find just the information you were seeking. Jung recognised that living from a coherent place within—where your subconscious and conscious minds are in a state of harmony—is something most people don't achieve within their lifetime. However, the newest research, such as that which underpins the techniques of change performance that I use in my work and am sharing with you in this book, make it possible to do just that—unite your subconscious and conscious minds harmoniously so that your entire life benefits as a result and you move into a state of high efficiency in achieving whatever you choose.

Here's an example of what I mean: I call this story 'Sophie Gets Her Man'. In one of my workshops there is an exercise where participants identify a large, overall life goal and undertake a process to gain clarity and specificity about it. We then identify the beliefs they need to integrate at the subconscious level to achieve this goal. Sophie's goal was a committed romantic relationship. Actually, what she really wanted, as she expressed it, was the man of her dreams. She diligently carried out the exercise and used the techniques for integrating the new beliefs into her subconscious. Within one month of taking my workshop, Sophie met her man. Her hobby is scuba diving, a new guy joined her diving club—and, as the saying goes, the rest is history. But the story doesn't end there. Two years later she was married and a little while later they had a beautiful baby girl. Was this meeting a coincidence? Or was Sophie now ready to recognise, meet and engage the man who turned out to be her ideal partner? I am convinced, as is she, that changing her subconscious programming made all the difference towards her realising her dream.

Here's one of the reasons why: your subconscious will filter your experiences to make links and associations only to things that have been programmed into it as being relevant to you. Have you ever been at a party and been fully engaged in a conversation and from a distant part of the room you hear your name? Although you may have been fully engrossed in your conversation, your subconscious mind with its 40-million-bit-per-second information processor heard your name and brought it to your conscious awareness for you to decide whether you needed to take any action or not.

Replacing outdated, self-sabotaging programs with new, self-supportive ones, such as those found in Appendix C at the back of this book, will help you gain more clarity on what you really want and need in your life. Your subconscious mind will, in effect, be a more efficient filter. The likelihood of achieving goals and dreams and creating the life you desire is astronomically higher when your subconscious is working with you, not against you.

The Subconscious Talks to Us through the Body

Your subconscious thinking can be detected through your body. For instance, in a study from the neuroscience department at the University of Iowa, two groups of people were asked to play a card game that could earn them money. There were four packs of cards they would use. The details of the game aren't important. What is important is that they didn't know that the packs were rigged: two of them were advantageous to their making money and the other two lessened their chances. The researchers monitored which packs the participants drew cards from, while also monitoring their skin temperature and conductance, which are markers of heightened arousal and stress. They also monitored the participants' attitudes and awareness of their progress in the game. Interestingly, after playing with all four packs, and before they became aware that two packs were disadvantageous, the participants' skin conductance responses were higher when they were pondering making a choice from the bad packs. This showed that consciously they did not know they were about to pull a card from a bad pack, but their skin conductance responses showed that at the subconscious level they were sceptical of those two packs. Their skin conductance revealed this suspicion before they actually drew any cards, providing a subtle inner warning that pulling from one of these two packs was a bad idea. If they had been able to listen to this inner voice or 'gut feeling', which often provides clues to its choices via the body, they would have increased their profit in the game.

Look at the image in Figure 4.2 overleaf. Can you spot the bumble bee, bird and ant?

Did you also spot anything else in the picture that is out of the ordinary, and perhaps even a bit shocking?

How about the word written in the negative white space between the lower part of the flower stalks?

Figure 4.2   *This image is used with kind permission from Subliminal Sex Flower Design: © August Bullock 1979. Artwork by Nelson Carrick. All Rights Reserved. Used with permission. From* The Secret Sales Pitch: An Overview of Subliminal Advertising *by August Bullock, Norwich Publishers, 2004. TheSecretSalesPitch.com.*

If you don't yet see it, look again. It's a word connected to the 'birds and the bees'. It's the word 'sex'.

Chances are that if a scientist were monitoring your skin conductance, he or she would have picked up a response indicating that your subconscious awareness registered that word, even if your conscious mind did not. Once you have recognised the word in the image consciously, you will always see it. But the point here is that your subconscious picks up huge amounts of information embedded in the environment that your conscious mind screens out as irrelevant or uncomfortable, especially when you are focused on a specific task, such as looking for a bee, bird or ant.

I've talked about how most of our subconscious programming takes place during childhood. However, it does not stop then. It continues throughout our life, much to the delight and profit of the advertising and marketing industries. Advertisers spend millions of dollars each year using psychological techniques that play at the subconscious level to entice you to take actions or buy products that you might not otherwise. They understand that it is the consumer's subconscious mind that makes most decisions, and they are experts at forming associations between your subconscious programming and their clients' products and services.

Most of us are exposed to more than 5000 marketing messages every day. Advertisers design their campaigns to emotionally influence the subconscious in a fleeting instant, with colour, words, images and music. Subliminal (meaning below your conscious threshold) advertising is a hugely popular method of reaching the subconscious, and we are exposed to hundreds of thousands of subliminal messages each year. Studies exploring subliminal perception show clearly how they influence subconscious processing and action. In one study, two groups of students were shown two different but similar pictures of trees. One group saw a picture only of the trees. The others saw the second image, which was doctored to also contain an artfully concealed duck. After studying their image, each group was asked to draw a nature scene and to label it. The group who had studied the trees that contained the subliminal duck image drew more ducks and related imagery, such as feathers, birds and water, as compared to the other group, who had studied the undoctored image.[6]

In another study, published in 1984 in the *Journal of Advertising*, researchers gathered two groups of participants, one shown advertisements with no subliminal images and the other shown advertisements containing sexually subliminal messages. The first doctored ad was for Marlboro Lights cigarettes, and it showed cowboys on horseback riding through rocky terrain. Subtly blended into the rocks was an image of a penis (yes, a penis). The second ad was for Chivas Regal whisky, and in the bottle a designer had skilfully and subtly blended the image of the back of a nude woman. Everyone in the study was hooked up to monitoring equipment, such as machines that recorded galvanic skin response, which measures stress levels and arousal through the electrical conductivity levels of the skin. Your skin conductivity will react even to subconscious arousal, which is part of the principle on which lie detector tests are based. Each group looked at the ads (one group the undoctored ads, the other group the ads containing the subliminal images) for only 30 seconds. The result was that the arousal response of the group who saw the advertisements containing the subliminal sexual images was 20% higher than for the group who saw the advertisements without the subliminal messages.[7]

Why do advertisers go to such lengths in their advertising? Because a stronger emotional subconscious association between an image and a brand/product causes millions of us to make purchasing choices for those products, choices we might not otherwise have made if we had been considering only price, quality and other more independent and impartial factors. Subliminal advertising can be very sneaky—and potentially manipulative—which is why many countries now ban it, even though that is quite tricky as by its very nature you do not know about it consciously.

Our consumer habits are a gold mine for researchers of subconscious action and motivation. Ask yourself why you are loyal to certain brands of products. You might think it is because you are a savvy shopper and are choosing on quality or price. But, like most people, a huge percentage of your decision making and brand loyalty is based on emotional subconscious thinking. Some of the reasons you are drawn to one product—or like its advertising—over another are subtle indeed. For example, in a study done to explore sincerity in advertising, researchers found that consumers unconsciously prefer advertisements where the models have characteristics of infants and that contain baby animals or human babies. This preference for the physical characteristics of infants or childhood anatomy, especially faces, is known as neotony. Neotonous characteristics include round eyes and high foreheads, characteristics that are believed to unconsciously trigger positive thoughts and feelings of sincerity, naïveté, innocence and honesty. Unsurprisingly, the consumers questioned were not consciously aware of the effect of neotony on their choices.

If you are still in doubt about the power of below-conscious-awareness perception, then try this exercise. Look at Figure 4.3

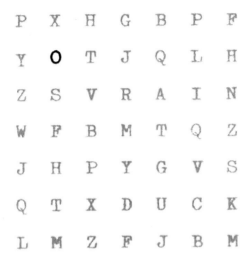

P   X   H   G   B   P   F

Y   **O**   T   J   Q   L   H

Z   S   V   R   A   I   N

W   F   B   M   T   Q   Z

J   H   P   Y   G   V   S

Q   T   X   D   U   C   K

L   M   Z   F   J   B   M

Figure 4.3

above for two seconds, then turn your eyes away. Pay attention to how you feel as well as to what you notice.

If you are like most people, you noticed right away that the letter O is bold black. Now look at Figure 4.4 overleaf for two seconds.

You probably noticed that the black bold letter is an E. But is that the only difference?

What you may not have noticed consciously, but many of you registered unconsciously, is that Figure 4.4 contains three provocative and emotionally charged words (one of which is even a largely forbidden word): 'F*CK', 'PAIN' and 'SEX'. Figure 4.3, in contrast, contains the words 'DUCK', 'RAIN' and 'SOX'. These images were used in an experiment, reported in the *Journal of Psychology* back in 1976, that sought to discern the power of subconscious information processing compared to conscious information processing. Here's how the study went and what it showed.[8]

Students were divided into two groups: one group was shown the image in Figure 4.3 and the other group the image in Figure 4.4. They were shown the images for a maximum of two seconds. The researchers used a camera to monitor the students'

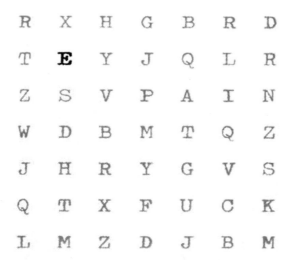

Figure 4.4   *Used with kind permission from Matrix Designs: From* The Secret Sales Pitch: An Overview of Subliminal Advertising *by August Bullock, Norwich Publishers, 2004. TheSecretSalesPitch. com. Referring to the original study: Somekh, D.E. (1976). The effect of embedded words in a brief visual display. British Journal of Psychology. 67(4): 529–35.*

eye movements. (They found that those two seconds were enough time for students to scan the entire image.) After the scan, they asked the students to look at an unrelated picture of an activity and to write about it, to describe what was going on in the picture, what might happen next according to the activity in the picture and so on. Amazingly, the students who had seen the image in Figure 4.4, the letter grid containing the hidden provocative words, were heavily influenced in their writing by the emotions of those words, as compared to the group who had scanned the image containing the emotionally neutral words. The stories of the 4.4 image group contained more conflict, loss, uncertainty and violence, and they used more unpleasant language as compared to the language of the 4.3 group. This result strongly suggests that at the subconscious level, the students who had seen the provocative words at a subliminal level were later emotionally reacting to them while engaged in a situation that was not in any way related (writing about a picture showing some mundane activity). They were not consciously aware that they had been influenced, but it showed up clearly in the stories they wrote.

Advertisers and others, from parents to politicians, rely on such subconscious tendencies to exert their influence. All of us are subject to such subconscious influence, and it is worth remembering this not only for ourselves but also for our children, who are exposed to extraordinary levels of media, especially violent media, such as television shows and movies and especially computer games. We can't really know how much the subliminal effect of the content carries over into their everyday, conscious lives. Here are several more example of ways in which consumers are influenced by subconscious programming:

❏ Identical products sell many more units if priced at £9.99 than £10.00. At a conscious level, the one penny difference is no big saving, but subconsciously it is thought to be a far better deal and an attractive saving.

❏ Consumers familiar with both a generic brand and a well-known brand of an over-the-counter medication insisted that they knew the two brands were identical except for price. Bizarrely, when they needed the products because they had severe symptoms the products would help ease, the same number of these consumers chose the higher-priced product.[9] Even more interesting is that if the medication was for a loved one, such as a child or spouse, purchasers nearly always chose the more expensive well-known brand instead of the generic, lower priced one. Subconsciously, these buyers had been programmed to make a strong association between the name recognition of the higher-priced brand with the feeling that it was more effective. Psychologically speaking, another factor is that people do not want to feel they are scrimping when it comes to caring for loved ones, so they buy the premium brand.

❏ Blind taste tests (where the drinkers did not know the names of the brands) of two beverages showed that more consumers preferred Beverage B to Beverage A. However, when the same

products were tested with the brands not hidden, the participants preferred Beverage A, which was a well-known brand, in
significant numbers over Beverage B, which was a generic
brand. This research showed the power of perception over taste
buds![10]

Here's a final, more extended example of subconscious influence.
In January 2007, Eli Hoddap, an astute assistant chef from
Chicago, was watching the hit television show *Iron Chef America*.
The show has fast-paced, timed cook-offs between competitors,
who are usually famous chefs, to create the best-tasting dishes
using a single main ingredient—the 'secret ingredient'—which is
not revealed until the beginning of the competition. As he was
enjoying the show, the sharp-eyed Eli caught a glimpse of something flash across the screen. As he was also recording the show
on his video machine, he was able to rewind the programme and
watch it again in slow motion, seeking to discover what the
flashed message or image was. To his surprise, he saw a
'McDonald's I'm Lovin' It' advertising tagline appear and then
disappear on the screen in just 1/30th of a second. Later, this flash
advertisement became the topic of public controversy, considered
as illegal or unfair subliminal advertising by many, although
McDonald's denied that it was deliberately using subliminal techniques. You can view the video on www.youtube.com and judge
for yourself.

    I won't belabour my point in this section, but the media are
masters of subconscious programming. They are so good that most
people do not believe they are influenced by it. However, television
is the plug-in drug. It is all pervasive, ultra-powerful and society
shaping. Television programming mostly pumps out fear, doom,
gloom, violence and false claims, 24 hours a day. Many people
think that because something is said on television or in the news-
papers it must be a true and accurate representation of how life is.
But most of the programming is paid for or sponsored by advertising, and the advertisers have their own profit-driven goals to
achieve.

We cannot be so naïve as to think that we are not being subconsciously influenced by their agendas and messages. Imagine the difference to your life and to society if day in and day out there was positive, uplifting programming and balanced news reports that focused some of their air time on what's right with the world. Imagine the difference to your frame of reference in the world if you were taking in positive stories of success and achievement, of happiness and compassion. Imagine the effect if instead of films and programmes focused on violence and killing, there were movies and broadcasts about the power of the human mind and how to access its potential, about how to expand awareness and engage innate healing abilities. What a different world we would create because what a different set of core beliefs we would all be living.

Updating and reprogramming your subconscious beliefs can not only lead to a dramatic increase in your personal vitality, happiness and success, but also contribute to positive societal and global change. We now have the knowledge from twenty-first-century science to make such changes at the level of our deepest personal belief systems. I have assisted thousands of people through my workshops and coaching programmes to experience new levels of awareness using techniques like the ones I am about to share with you.

To highlight just how amazingly powerful our mind, beliefs and perceptions are on our physical body, in the next chapter we will look at some breathtaking evidence...

Key Points

- ❏ Aligning your subconscious mind with your conscious goals dramatically increases your ability to manifest your goals.
- ❏ Your subconscious mind will filter for links and associations to things that have been programmed into it.
- ❏ Advertising is aimed at making associations to influence your subconscious mind.
- ❏ In today's fast-paced world updating your subconscious mind is crucial for your success.

5

CAN THE MIND REALLY AFFECT MATTER?

What you believe to be true is true within certain limits which itself is a belief. In the province of the mind there are no real limits.

Dr John Lilly

Towards the end of the nineteenth century, William James, the father of modern psychology, said, 'No mental modification ever occurs which is not accompanied or followed by a bodily change.'[1] More recently, Dr Norman Cousins summarised the modern view of the mind–body interaction as 'belief becomes biology'.[2] One powerful way to explore how your beliefs affect your biology is through conventional medical studies, which must always take into account a phenomenon called the placebo effect. Most of us have heard of the placebo effect, although most of us also misunderstand what it is really all about. 'A placebo, as used in research, is an inactive substance or procedure used as a control in an experiment. The placebo effect is the measurable, observable, or felt improvement in health not attributable to an actual treatment.'[3]

During the research for this book, one of the most amazing examples I came across of the power of beliefs and perceptions to affect the physical body came from Stewart Wolf. Dr Wolf did a double-blind study with pregnant women who were suffering from nausea and vomiting. He divided the group in two and gave one group an anti-sickness medicine and the other group a placebo, a substance that had no known therapeutic effect on nausea. The women in the anti-sickness medicine group improved— their nausea was gone. However, many of the women in the placebo group also found relief.[4] This is the placebo effect at work—in this case, women who believed the treatment would relieve their nausea were cured of their symptoms, even though, unbeknown to them, the treatment they were taking was medically useless for nausea.

There are literally thousands of such studies that demonstrate the power of belief to affect the physical body, and we will look at many of the most impressive in this chapter. But let's go back to the study of the pregnant women suffering from nausea. There's more to this story!

The study has a second part—the really stunning aspect of it. To explore the placebo effect even further, Dr Wolf gave the placebo group another medication, which he characterised as a 'new, strong, very effective anti-sickness' drug. This time not just some of the women, but all of them experienced relief from nausea and vomiting.[5] What was this amazing new pharmaceutical? It's called Ipecac and check this, Ipecac is a very powerful drug used in hospital emergency rooms to induce vomiting! Just the strong belief that they were taking an amazing new anti-sickness drug was enough to totally reverse the chemical action of this drug on their bodies. Think about this result for a moment. The women's belief in the doctor and expectation about the effect of the drug not only totally eradicated their symptoms, it completely reversed the chemical action of a purgative drug in their bodies. I don't know about you, but for me this study is among the most convincing evidence yet that our minds are amazingly powerful. To paraphrase a popular saying in the hard sciences, incredible claims require incredibly reliable proof. So let's keep looking at that proof via studies of the placebo effect that reveal our minds as being one of the most critical factors to the state of our health, and by extension to the state of our entire lives and the potential we express.

Have you ever had a sore gum after some dental treatment? Morphine is an extremely powerful painkiller—can our mind be as powerful? In a study of pain after dental surgery, patients were given either intravenous morphine or a saline placebo. If they were told that the saline was a powerful new painkiller, they got just as much relief as the patients who received morphine. Once again, the only explanation is that their belief in the treatment translated into their bodies responding as if they were getting an effective treatment.[6]

Old Wisdom, New Wisdom

Let's look at a different kind of placebo effect study. It's another one that throws into question all we have been told about ourselves, our bodies, our health and our abilities to influence our reality. Back in 1979, psychologist Dr Ellen Langar, then at Harvard University, and her colleagues devised an ingenious experiment to test the power of perceptions on the state of the physical body.[7] Langar and her team hypothesised that they could reverse the biological ageing of a group of men aged 75 and older. That's right—they were seeking to reverse physiological ageing. We determine our age by our birthday: you are 25, or 36, or 42 or 88. But another way to assess age is via physiological markers in the body and the cognitive function of the brain. Not all 56 year olds are in the same condition: some are physiologically older or younger than others who are their chronological age. So the intention of Langar and her team was to see if a person's psychological perception of him- or herself as old or young could directly influence the biological ageing process.

The experiment involved only men, who were taken to live together at a retreat centre for one week. Before being taken there, they were all thoroughly evaluated and tested for short-term memory, cognition, hearing, taste, sight, posture, perception and physical strength (which are many of the markers that help determine biological age, as opposed to chronological age). They also had their pictures taken.

The retreat centre was specially created to be a time capsule from 1959—everything in it, from the furniture to the appliances to the books and magazines to the music playing on the stereo, was indicative of 1959. The men were not allowed to take anything with them, such as recent family photos, personal papers, books etc., that would remind them of the current time (1979), so they were thoroughly immersed in a world 20 years in the past. They were also carefully counselled and coached to act as if it were 20 years earlier. They were to discuss their wives and families as if it were 1959, and pretend they were still working at the job or in the career of that year. The staff were very particular and paid attention to the tiniest detail. To all intents and purposes, these men were time-travelling back to a time when they were 20 years younger.

As any good study must be structured, there was also a control group of men who were housed in another part of the retreat centre. The centre looked modern and current (1979) and the men were told to simply enjoy themselves as if they were on holiday. They had no instructions about dates, year or time, so they were more or less just enjoying a week of retreat, with everything normal for 1979. As a control group, they would provide data about whether relaxing in a non-stressful atmosphere had any impact on the biological markers of ageing.

At the end of the week, all the men were tested once again for the markers of biological ageing, and their pictures were re-taken. The before and after pictures were shown to a group of independent 'judges' who were asked to compare the two photos and say in which one the man looked younger and to guess how many years younger he appeared to be. The judges did not know the reason they were being asked to compare the pictures, as they were unaware of the experimental set-up. This way they would be totally impartial. Almost unanimously, the impartial judges said the men in the post-retreat photos for the time-capsule group were younger—by an average of three years—than their pre-retreat photos. There was no difference for the non-time-capsule group. The scientists then went on to do post-retreat physiological evaluations. Amazingly, the bodies of the men who had been living as if it were 1959 actually grew younger! For example, the lengths of the fingers, which tend to reduce or shrink with age, had increased, as had their hand grip strength. Their vision and hearing acuities improved. Nearly half of this group of men experienced an increase in IQ. As astounding as it seems, Dr Langar provided an opportunity for these men to be psychologically 20 years younger, and their bodies followed suit. Their minds literally turned back their body clocks. There were no such changes in biological markers for the men in the non-time-capsule group.

Another study on ageing was conducted by Professor of Preventative Medicine Alexander Leaf, then of the Harvard Medical School. He travelled the globe researching cultures that had many healthy centenarians—people who have reached their hundredth birthday. He even found many people who were between 110 years old and 115 years old and still in good health. He gathered massive amounts of data about them and their internal and external environments, including the weather, their diet and their genetic dispositions. His conclusions were that none of these factors made a difference to how healthy they remained at such an advanced age. There was only one common denominator—their cultural beliefs about ageing. In all of these cultures, elders are greatly respected, so that growing old is an honour. The older you are, the wiser and more useful you are to your community. These elders were surrounded by family members, peers and a culture at large that valued them and their life experience. The collective perception of ageing had a dramatic effect on the individual's biological expression of ageing, keeping them vigorous, alert and active, sometimes well into their second century.[8]

We've all been told what to expect as we age—that it's an inevitable process of our bodies and minds slowing down and even deteriorating. These studies and others show the lie to that belief. Let's now look at some other 'perceived wisdom' that is turning out not to be totally reliable or even true.

Pushing the Boundaries of Belief

There is one area where evidence of the placebo effect would provide extremely compelling evidence of its existence and effectiveness—surgery. It is common knowledge in medicine that a placebo has no effect on surgery, whose effectiveness is entirely independent of our psychology. After all, going into the body with a scalpel is a precise and unambiguous event. The patient is usually under anaesthesia and there are not many variables from the person's life, belief system or perceptions that affect how skilful a surgeon is or how he or she does the job. Although a patient's attitude, beliefs and perceptions can influence the experience of post-surgical pain and the speed of recovery, they have no impact on the actual operation itself. Or do they? One doctor decided to find out.

Orthopaedic surgeon Bruce Moseley, of the Baylor School of Medicine, wondered which component of the arthroscopy (knee surgery) operation he performed was the most effective and beneficial for his patients, as there are at least two different procedures he could do while working inside a patient's damaged knee: he could shave damaged knee cartilage or flush floating cartilage debris out of the knee cavity. Both approaches were very common, but there was no data on which was most effective. So, Dr Moseley decided to try to find out.[10]

He consulted with the hospital director and others, who told him that to find an answer he would have to conduct a double-blind study, which would need two groups of patients—each group getting one or the other of the procedures—and a third group to serve as a control. The control group would have to think they had surgery, but not actually have anything done to their damaged knee. Dr Moseley was surprised at the need for a control group, which would make it possible for the study to factor in the placebo effect. He said, 'All good surgeons know that there is no placebo in surgery.'[11]

But he went ahead and managed to arrange for such a complex study to be carried out. There were three groups of patients—all comprised of men who had greatly reduced activity levels because of knee damage, with some of them even finding the need to use wheelchairs. Each man in each group underwent the arthroscopic surgery, with one group having the cartilage shaved, another having their knee cavity flushed, and the third group being brought into the operating room but not actually having either of the procedures. Here's what happened for the third group—the control group—during their 'fake' surgery.

To make them believe they were undergoing the procedure, everything was done normally. They were sedated, Dr Moseley made the standard incisions in their knee, but then he did nothing surgical. He faked the operation. He positioned the monitor that he used to see inside the knee and all other equipment exactly where he would have if he were actually going to operate. He played a video of a real operation on the monitor in case a patient were watching. (Although the patients were sedated, they were not totally unconscious and could watch an actual operation on the monitor; in this case it was all arranged so that they wouldn't be able to know it was not their knee in the video.) After 40 minutes he stitched up the small incisions he had made in the knee as if he had performed the operation as usual. Every last detail was accounted for so that the control group could not know they had not received real knee surgery.

The results were totally unexpected. All three groups improved equally well, although according to received wisdom the men who had not had anything done to their knees should have been in the same debilitating condition as before the study. But they improved too! They regained motion, had less pain, were able to resume life activities—from walking without pain to playing basketball with their grandkids—that many had given up because of their knee problem. Even two years later, when the men in the placebo control group were told that nothing had been done to their knee, they still retained the benefits. Further follow-up six years later found the benefits to be lasting, with no relapses.

This study and its years-long aftermath was a spectacular display of the power of the placebo effect. Dr Moseley concluded:

> *My skill as a surgeon had no benefit on these patients. The entire benefit of surgery for osteoarthritis of the knee was down to the placebo effect.*

One of the patients in the control group, Tim Perez, told the reporters of the Discovery Health Channel for a programme on the placebo effect that detailed this study and interviewed Dr Moseley and some of the patients:

> *Boy, was I surprised to know that it was the placebo. I couldn't believe it. How is this possible? Well, in this world anything is possible when you put your mind to it. I know that your mind can work miracles.*

The placebo effect is not a psychological effect only. At one time, it was thought by the general public to mean that their disease and symptoms were all in their minds, and they were making themselves sick. That view is outdated and inaccurate. The modern concept of the placebo is one of optimism and wonder—that we have self-healing capabilities that we have not even begun to learn to harness. The placebo effect shows us that biology is still an infant science, as is medicine, and that we have a lot to learn. Emerging science on the placebo effect and the power of our minds means that one day we might not have to rely as heavily as we do on pharmaceuticals and their nasty side effects. We can use our mind power and potential to activate our body's own natural chemicals to do the job that synthetic chemicals and pharmaceuticals attempt to do.

Study after study is reminding us that somewhere in the deep recesses of our bodies, linked intimately with our thoughts, perceptions and beliefs, is a mechanism for healing ourselves. For instance, recent MRI brain scans taken of people on Prozac for depression showed changes in the brain when a patient took Prozac but showed the same changes when they received a placebo and just thought it was Prozac.[12] Similarly, when Parkinson's patients were given an anti-Parkinson's drug, their tremors were reduced and their brains increased their production and use of dopamine, a natural brain chemical that helps alleviate Parkinson's symptoms. However, when patients were given a placebo but thought it was the drug, the tremors also reduced and the brain still released the same amount of dopamine in the same areas.[13] The pressing question is, if the drugs weren't necessary, what was relieving them of their symptoms? The answer appears to be that the patients' own belief systems and thought patterns activated what we might call the body's own 'intelligence and healing wisdom', so their bodies worked naturally to deal with the disease symptoms. Many recent studies have shown that most of the major anti-depression drugs in use today are no more effective than a placebo. However, as former pharmaceutical scientist Dr David Hamilton says,

> *The drugs probably do work, although we don't absolutely know for sure, but when we believe in a drug, whatever the drug is for, our own natural healing capacity kicks in.*[14]

The revolution that is coming in medicine and healthcare will be based on better activating and using our natural self-healing capabilities.

I can guess that as you read the placebo effect studies, you were asking yourself, 'Well, if I believe something is working and that makes my body respond, then isn't the opposite also true? Can't my beliefs make me sick or stop a treatment from working?' The answer is yes. The placebo effect works both ways, which brings me to a discussion of its twin—the nocebo effect. The nocebo effect is the term used to describe the harmful, unpleasant or undesirable reactions from a person's pessimistic belief—the exact opposite of the placebo effect.

Here are a few examples of the nocebo effect to give you a brief idea of how it works.

❑ In a study, a group of 34 college students were told that a mild electrical current was being passed through their heads, which might induce a headache as an effect. There was no actual electrical current passed through their heads, yet over 66% of the 34 students developed headaches.[15]

❑ In a study of people with asthma, a group of patients breathed in a vapour that researchers told them was a chemical irritant or allergen. Nearly half of the patients experienced breathing problems, with a dozen developing full-blown asthma attacks. They were 'treated' with a substance they believed to be a bronchial dilating medicine, and they recovered immediately. In actuality, both the 'irritant' and the 'medicine' were a nebulised (reduced to a fine spray) saltwater solution.[16]

❑ Japanese researchers tested 57 high-school boys for their sensitivity to allergens. The boys filled out questionnaires about past experiences with plants, including lacquer trees, which can cause itchy rashes, much like poison oak and poison ivy do. Boys who reported having severe reactions to lacquer trees were blindfolded. Researchers brushed one arm with leaves from a lacquer tree but told the boys they were chestnut tree leaves. The scientists stroked the other arm with chestnut tree leaves but said the foliage came from a lacquer tree. Within minutes the arm the boys believed to have been exposed to the poisonous tree began to react, turning red and developing a bumpy, itchy rash. In most cases, but not all, the arm that had contact with the actual allergen did not react.[17]

In each of these studies, it was the person's beliefs—and fears and expectations—that created the nocebo effect. This effect has profound implications, and we would all do well to pay attention to our beliefs and expectations in terms of our health, for if you don't have confidence in a treatment, it is likely that it won't be that effective for you.

Professor William Tiller sums up the power of our minds and bodies in his ground-breaking book *PsychoEnergetic Science*,

> *Every change in the human physiological state is accompanied by an appropriate change in the mental emotional state, conscious or unconscious, and conversely every change in the human mental emotional state, conscious or unconscious, is accompanied by an appropriate change in the physiological state.*

Here are a couple of examples from my own life that brought this truth home to me. Such experiences are part of the reasons why I am so dedicated to teaching belief-change and consciousness-expansion techniques to people around the world.

Mind over Matter: Dice, Seeds, Lights and Spoonbending

Here's a belief-shattering experience I had: spoon bending. I can hear you now: 'That's just a magic trick, isn't it?' Here is what I experienced. In the autumn of 2002, I visited the Monroe Institute, an organisation devoted to research about consciousness and expanded human abilities that is located in Virginia (USA). I participated in a six-day psychokinesis workshop. Psychokinesis is the term used to describe mind affecting matter and, more specifically, moving matter without the use of any physical force. The workshop was run by Professor of Psychology Joe Gallenberger. The nature of this workshop was not dryly scientific, but was a way for the general public to explore the topic in an engaging and participatory way.

In the group there were about 20 people, from all over the world. We met each morning for a meditation and to be briefed about the events planned for that day. Many of the experiential aspects of exploring our consciousness involved the use of a sound technology developed and patented by the Institute's founder, Robert Monroe, called Hemi-Sync™. It is designed to heighten states of consciousness by shifting brain waves and creating coherence between the heart, brain, mind and body.

About five times per day we would go to our rooms, where we each had a sound-proofed sleeping cabin in which we would stretch out and put on headphones to listen to the special Hemi-Sync frequencies that helped induce the expanded state of awareness. Part of the process was to hold the intention to quieten your internal mental chatter and foster heart-based feelings of love, joy, kindness and appreciation.

After we spent some time attaining and experiencing these heightened states of consciousness, we would regroup in another part of the Institute and experiment with our abilities to influence physical matter using only our minds. We had a lot of fun playing mind games, such as trying to influence the dice in games of craps so that they would come up a certain desired number. Dr Joe, as we called him, was a statistician *extraordinaire*, and he recorded the results of many, many trials and showed us how the results showed every participant was able to influence the dice beyond chance odds. (By the way, this is a common 'mind over matter' experiment. Rigorous studies conducted over the period 1935 to 1987, involving more than 2500 people trying to influence more than 2.6 million dice throws in more than 148 different experiments, showed that they are able to do so to a staggering statistical probability: the odds against chance were 10^{96} to 1! That's 10 with 96 zeroes after it! Control experiments, where no mental influence was used, resulted in chance expectations.[18])

We did other interesting experiments, such as trying to influence seed germination by sending one pot of seeds loving energy and talking to it as a friend or as if it were a baby we were nurturing (if my friends could only have seen me sitting out in the sun talking to my pot of seeds they would have definitely thought I had gone off the deep end). We ignored the other control pot of seeds. The well-loved seeds sprouted very quickly. In five days, they showed 200% more growth than the seeds we had ignored.

We even made a neon light tube, which was unplugged from any source of electrical current, glow in our hands, just by holding it and expanding loving energy. Sound crazy? Well, it worked! Okay, we spent a lot of time in meditation and using the Hemi-Sync technology to 'prime' our minds and expand our state of consciousness. But preparation or not, all of these experiences happened. OK, on to the spoons.

They saved the spoon-bending activity for our last evening. This was the one we had all been waiting for! By this time we had each had about 25 Hemi-Sync meditation-type sessions, and the whole group was in a highly expanded state of awareness. We were in a state of 'flow'. In fact, as we gathered together on this final evening, it was as if we were not individuals at all but a single powerful energy field.

The bag of spoons came out and each of us selected one, as music played in the background of the room. We quietened our minds and focused on attaining a heart-centred, loving feeling. As we did this, we held the shaft of a spoon in one hand whilst applying minimal pressure on the round part of the spoon. Our intention was to realise—to believe—that at the most fundamental level—at the subatomic level—both we and our spoons were made of nothing but vortices of pure energy.

I was so fully in the zone I had no doubt I could bend my spoon without any force, by simply using my intent. Before long my spoon was changing shape, the round part drooping as if the metal had been heated and softened. So were the spoons of others. People of all ages and backgrounds were bending spoons with next to no physical effort. It was a spectacular experience! (Only two people of the 20 failed to bend their spoons with their minds. In the debrief afterwards, they admitted that they had not believed from the start of the exercise that they could do it.) The events of this week-long course left me with two certainties: the mind can influence matter, and the key to this was not to think too much about it, in fact the less you think the better, and accessing a loving, open, receptive, heart-centred state is crucial to achieving that influence.

But you don't have to take my word that our mind can influence matter. This phenomenon has been the focus of tightly controlled experiments over many decades. Your mind is a force to be reckoned with, and it can be a tool to influence your environment—and your life—in ways we are only beginning to understand.

The power is in the heart, which turns out to be the key to switching on higher brain functions and abilities. In the next chapter we'll take a very quick look at what we need to know about our brain and heart as they relate to changing and updating our beliefs and maximising our potential.

Key Points

❏ Your health is significantly influenced by your mindset.
❏ Your mind is so powerful it can actually reverse ageing.
❏ Psychokinesis, 'mind affecting matter', is a real phenomenon.
❏ You have untapped abilities waiting to be awakened.

6

HOW TO UNLOCK YOUR BRAIN'S POTENTIAL

This is my simple religion. There is no need for temples; no need for complicated philosophy. Our own brain, our own heart is our temple.

Dalai Lama

For many years it was believed that the brain was hardwired and fixed and that its growth was fully established by the time we reach adulthood. Research from neuroscience now shows us this is not true. We now know that our brain can continually learn, change and create new neural circuitry throughout our life. The brain's adaptability and capacity for change are called 'neuroplasticity'.

The major brain cells that allow the brain to be an information processor are called neurons, and we have about 100 billion of them. Neurons contain axons, which carry electrochemical messages, and dendrites, which are branching structures that reach out to connect with other neurons. Between neurons are tiny junctions called synapses, across which electrochemical signals are sent from neuron to neuron. There may be between 1000 and 10,000, with some estimates as high as 30,000, synapses connecting any two neurons, ultimately forming a vast network of neuronal connections called 'neuronets'. You can think of neuronets as electromagnetic and electrochemical superhighways along which information is sent from the brain to the body, and vice versa. As we integrate new belief systems, we form new neuronets, which we strengthen and develop by taking action towards our goals, giving us more choices and enhancing and expanding our abilities.

How Powerful Is your Brain?

To get an idea of how powerful your brain is, imagine every single person on earth, all 7 billion of us, with a hand-held calculator performing a calculation every five seconds for sixty hours. Okay, got your head around that image? The world's most powerful computers, called supercomputers, can perform the same amount of 7 billion calculations every five seconds for sixty hours in just one second! That's an accomplishment that blows our minds, until we realise that it would take three of these supercomputers linked together to map the connections to just one single neuronet firing in the human brain.[1] A piece of brain the size of a grain of salt contains approximately 100,000 neurons and a billion synapses. That is a lot of processing power. The total number of permutations and combinations of brain connections, and hence activity, is almost infinite. As Dr Andrew Newburg says,

> *We have astonishing potential to change the autopilot behaviours and patterns we have fallen into. Using the right tools and intentions, the potential for change within our nervous system, within our entire physiology is tremendous.*[2]

In 1980, there was a case reported in the prestigious journal *Science* where during a routine medical examination a student at Sheffield University was found to have virtually no brain.[3] The average-size cortex measures approximately 4 inches, but this student's cortex measured less than a millimetre thick. He still had an IQ of 126 and received a first-class degree in mathematics. His case and others show us how plastic—that is, adaptable—our brain is: how one part can compensate for other parts, and how much processing capacity there is in only small sections of the brain.

The brain is basically a threefold structure that grows from the bottom up as it develops (see Figure. 6.1). First there is the brainstem or hind brain; then the mid brain, which is also known as the limbic system or mammalian or emotional brain (containing the amygdala and hippocampus); and then there is the neocortex or forebrain (the 'thinking brain'). The neocortex is split into two

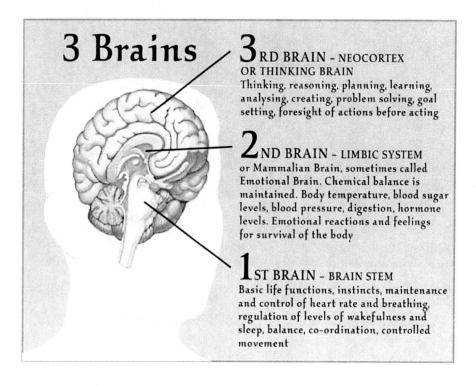

Figure 6.1 *The three major structures of the human brain and some of their functions.*

halves, a left and right hemisphere. Research pioneered by Dr Paul Maclean suggests that the three brains amount to three interconnected biological computers. Each possesses its own intelligence, subjectivity, sense of time and space, memory and other functions.[4]

The amygdala is an almond-shaped group of neurons that is situated deep in the limbic brain. Its primary role is alerting the body in survival situations. It also helps to correlate different emotional charges to your long-term memories. If anything in your environment reminds your subconscious mind/memory banks of a past experience that was threatening or felt uncomfortable, your amygdala will activate, sending your body into the survival response of fight or flight. Back when we were primitive beings exposed to the dangers of the environment, it was appropriate for us to respond to these flight-or-fight signals. If a tiger were coming at you, you would want to flee back to your cave to safety! But in today's modern world, you are not subject to many such life-or-death threats. Your amygdala, however, still responds to perceived threats, which more often than not are psychological rather than physical. Your emotions are constantly provoked—from anger to frustration to shame and guilt—as you negotiate the complexities of your busy days and complex relationships. Today, we call this response 'stress'. The constant pressure of stress on your system is as real as the sudden flow of chemicals that sent your primitive ancestors fleeing from tigers, and stress can wear you down, affecting your health and state of well-being. When under stress, your critical thinking and decision making are diminished, and you are more likely to act irrationally. As you clear your memory banks of outdated perceptions and update your subconscious programming with new, empowering beliefs, however, your body can react better to changes in the environment and you experience enhanced mental and emotional health and performance.

The cortex is the king of your brain. It is very large in humans compared to the rest of the animal world, which explains our higher thinking capacities, especially self-awareness. The frontal lobes are the most highly evolved area of the human brain. Your frontal lobes enable you to direct your attention, initiate behaviours, reason and rationalise. Frontal lobe activity is also crucial to helping you inhibit impulsive acts.

Although you now have a better understanding of your basic brain function, don't be fooled into thinking that you know more about your psychology. While conventional biology tells us our thinking—and really everything non-tangible about us that makes us the unique individuals that we are—is an emergent property of the brain, the leading edge of science shows us that our consciousness does not arise from brain chemistry. It is something different, as discussed previously in this book: consciousness is an independent state that is a flow of energy and information that connects us to the cosmos. Still, whatever your belief in terms of your brain's relationship to your consciousness, I suspect you will agree that learning to minimise stress is a good thing. What follows is a quick and effective technique for relieving stress and enhancing your performance.

Mind–Body Stress-Clearing Technique

Anytime you feel stressed, try this simple but powerful technique:

1. Rub your hands together vigorously for five seconds.
2. Then place your thumbs on your temples and the four fingers of each hand just above your eyebrows in the middle of your forehead.
3. Pull lightly to the sides of the head repeatedly for five to ten seconds so that you stretch the skin on your forehead. You are activating your emotional neurovascular reflexes which assist in balancing your emotional energy. Your brain will instantly increase the electrochemical activity in your frontal lobes, and the heat from your hand will draw blood away from your limbic system into your frontal cortex, allowing you to relax and make better decisions.

Give it go now by thinking of something that stresses you and trying this technique for yourself.

Your brain's cortex, as I said, is split into two halves: a left and right hemisphere. Each hemisphere has its own unique overall functions, which allow you to perceive the world in different ways. (See Figure 6.2.) Generally speaking, the left hemisphere is the seat of intellect in the guise of logic and reasoning, especially as the seat of ideas that are communicated through language. The right hemisphere is the seat of creativity and holistic thinking. It encodes for spatial reasoning and links you to the world through the medium of your feelings. Throughout your life, you will tend to develop dominance in one hemisphere over the other, which can limit you in how much of your potential and wisdom you can access in each moment. As a sweeping generalisation, if you grew up in a household where your creative and artistic talents were emphasised and where you were supported in trusting your feelings, imagination and intuition, your right hemisphere may be well developed and your left not so. Alternatively, if you grew up in a household where logic, structure and linear processes were the main ways of perceiving the world, your left hemisphere may have dominance in your

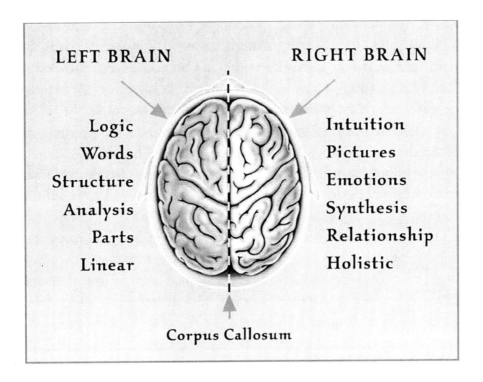

Figure 6.2 *The two hemispheres of your cortex have their own unique functions, bestowing different gifts. Generally speaking, the left hemisphere is the seat of logic and reasoning, whereas the right hemisphere is the seat of intuition and creativity.*

life. Interestingly, the hemispheric connections do not become fully mature until about the age of ten. When both sides of your brain are developed equally and so working together harmoniously, you have a very different view of the world than if one hemisphere is dominant.

As another generalisation, the western world has a heavy bias in the left hemispheric way of functioning, relying as it does on facts and science, logic and reasoning. I see the effects of this dominance especially in my corporate training seminars. Often the corporate mindset is so fixed on systems and processes that there often is little room for employees to express their creative and intuitive abilities. Managers are fixated on their employees 'doing things the right way' (which usually means the way things have always been done), and so they tend to value fidelity to the status quo over the risk-taking behaviours of change and innovation. Our educational systems also are heavily biased towards developing our left hemispheric talents, focusing as they do on consensual knowledge, facts,rote learning, science and mathematics, and less on creative expression, artistic exploration and out-of-the-box thinking.

The two hemispheres of the brain are connected by a band of fibres called the corpus callosum. This bridge allows information to be shared between the hemispheres, which fosters holistic thinking and optimised performance. The main point here is that for optimal integration of new belief systems, you need to access the activity of your frontal cortex and make sure you have achieved an integrated coherence of the left and right hemispheres, which creates a 'whole brain state'. Achieving this coherence is part of my Gamma Belief-Change Technique and the Gamma Brain Technique©, which I will share in a later chapter.

Professor Christopher M. Bache, in his book *Dark Night, Early Dawn,* tells us:

> *When the brain's hemispheres are phase-locked and work as one, a number of known benefits result, including heightened awareness, improved recall, enhanced self-programming flexibility, and increased creativity—in short, you increase your capacity for super learning.*

I only want to cover what is relevant to us about beliefs in this book, so I won't talk more about the power and beauty of brain function. There are scores of informative books about it. What I do want to spend some time exploring is a new subject that you may never have heard about—neurocardiology, which is uncovering exciting new information about how your heart may be equally important to your brain—or, in some respects, even more important—in the way your body works and the quality of your emotional life. This is an important factor in the Gamma Belief Change Technique©.

Your Heart Is the Key

Most of us think of the heart as a pump that propels blood around the body. That's certainly what I was taught in physiology classes at college. This is true, of course, but researchers at the leading edge of science are telling us it is so much more than a mere pump. The trouble is, this information is not widely known.

Traditionally, we think of the brain as the central computer of the body. It receives information from the five physical senses and sends information signals to the body to produce the desired actions and to drive physiological functions. I suspect that few of you know that your heart is an organ that can learn, remember, feel and sense independently of your brain! It's true. In fact, the research that has shown the heart to be a sensory organ led to the formation of a new medical discipline called neurocardiology, which is the study of the connections and communication between the nervous system and heart. This new area of study is revealing amazing facts about the heart.

In 1991, one of the pioneers in this field, Dr J Andrew Armour, of Dalhousie University in Canada, showed evidence that the heart has its own independent nervous system, which has been termed the 'brain in the heart', that has more than 40,000 neurons in it, as many as are found in some areas of the brain.[5] Why would the heart need brain cells? Scientific evidence has shown that the heart sends emotional and intuitive information signals to the brain and body, and that it can learn, remember, feel and sense.[6] Interestingly the heart sends more information to the brain than the brain does to the heart.

In a truly mind-boggling set of experiments, discussed in an article in the *Journal of Alternative and Complementary Medicine* in 2004, Dr Rollin McCraty from the Heartmath Institute—a leading-edge research centre for the scientific study of heart coherence and its health benefits and of other aspects of this revolutionary new science of the heart—found that the heart seems to 'know' the emotional future. That is, it is precognitively able to sense the emotional 'flavour' of events that may soon happen and reacts to that information before we actually experience the event and thus feel a significant emotion. In short, your heart senses intuitively, and then it conveys this information to the brain to prepare you for a response. I know that's hard to believe, so let me briefly explain the experiments.

Participants were each seated before a computer on which flashed randomly selected pictures. There were two types of pictures: those with neutral emotional content (such as a basket of fruit or a landscape) and those with heightened emotional content (such as erotic scenes or images of gruesome car crashes or autopsies). The participants were hooked up to equipment that monitored their heart beat, skin conductivity, brain-wave patterns, and other measures of nervous system and organ function. Baseline measures of these physiological parameters were taken. The participants did not do anything but sit and watch the computer screen, on which were flashed a series of pictures, spaced six seconds apart, with blank spans in between. The pictures were chosen at random by the computer. When the session was over, researchers had a record of which pictures were shown and in what order and the recordings of the participants' internal bodily responses during the session. What they discovered when they processed their data from the experiments was entirely unexpected.

The participants' hearts (and their other bodily responses) responded in a way that correlated with the emotional effect of the pictures (arousal for the emotionally charged pictures or calm baseline measures for the emotionally neutral ones). This was normal and expected. What was astounding was that their hearts responded seconds before their brains did! In fact the heart was the first part of their physiology to react to the stimulus. It sent input to the brain, instead of vice versa, which goes against the standard biological model that the brain is the command centre of the body. What was truly mind-boggling was that the heart responded (according to the monitoring equipment) even before a picture flashed on the computer screen. It appeared to know what was coming—it displayed what is called 'precognition'. If the picture that was going to display, but hadn't yet, was one of the gruesome ones, the heart showed an arousal response, and sent preparatory information to the brain so that the rest of the body could get ready as well.

Sometimes this happened up to 6 seconds before the picture flashed on the screen!

This series of experiments has deep implications for how our bodies work and how we are connected to the world outside of us. At the very least, it shows how we all respond subconsciously to input before we do consciously, and that our hearts play a significant role in our emotional lives. Dr McCraty summarised his findings as follows:

> *Of greatest significance here is our major finding: namely… evidence that the heart is directly involved with the processing of information about a future emotional stimulus seconds before the body actually experiences the stimulus… What is truly surprising about the result is the fact that the heart appears to play a direct role in the perception of future events, at the very least it implies that the brain does not act alone in this regard.*[7]

Studies such as this one may help explain all those metaphors and aphorisms about our heart and emotions: 'It breaks my heart'. 'Listen to your heart'. 'Follow your heart'. When we act from our heart centre we may be following the wisdom of our bodies. At a minimum, we are able to gain a different perspective on people, events and perceptions.

When you feel angry, frustrated or stressed, your heart rhythms reflect the state of your being. In this case, they would move away from a smooth, coherent pattern, becoming more erratic and random, like looking at a graph of an earthquake. This incoherent pattern causes a release of stress hormones, such as adrenaline and cortisol, which dampen the activity of the higher centres of your brain, including the neocortex, which is responsible for conscious thinking and what we think of as the 'wisdom' centre since it is active in decision making. You may have noticed in the past that when you fly into anger or intense stress, your ability to solve problems or think clearly is diminished. That's because when you perceive a situation as stressful, your body shunts blood to where it is most needed, which is to the lower, more primitive areas of your brain that put you into a flight-or-fight response. In contrast, when you experience feelings of appreciation, love, joy and kindness or just simply feeling relaxed and happy, your heart goes into a rhythm that is highly ordered and coherent, and your brain's cortex experiences heightened activity, allowing for more awareness. This is a state in which you can more easily make wise choices and integrate new, more positive beliefs and perceptions.

Mind-Body Heart-Brain Coherence Technique

1. Whenever you feel a stress response, immediately rub your hands together vigorously for 5–10 seconds and place one palm of your hand over your heart area and the other palm on your forehead. Focus your breath as if you are breathing through your heart area for five comfortably deep, slow breaths, focusing on the sensation of your palm on your body.
2. At the same time, think of something that makes you feel peaceful, loving or happy. Perhaps picture your spouse, child or a beloved pet. Or recall a memory of a wonderful holiday, event or personal interaction that makes you feel peaceful, joyful, appreciative or grateful. Use all your senses to re-experience that occasion as fully as possible. Doing so will change your heart rhythm from one of decoherence to one of coherence, and your whole body will change as a result, for the heart sends messages to your body just as surely as your brain does.

Within seconds of starting the above exercise, you will be shifting your heart rhythms into a more harmonious and health-enhancing pattern and also stimulating the higher centres of your brain. This is a wonderful exercise to do before you enter a meeting or give a public speech—or do anything else that is stressful for you—as it helps you to relax, increase your whole-brain functioning, and enhance your mood. This type of exercise is what is called a 'sincere appreciation technique', and it has been shown to change the chemical state of the body, especially as it relates to increasing levels of DHEA, which is an anti-ageing hormone, and to reducing the stress hormone cortisol. Howard Martin, of the HearthMath Institute in California, says,

> *A coherent body–mind system is highly efficient and highly ordered, meaning less waste of energy. There is improved respiration, digestion, better perceptions, increased reaction times and an improved visual field.*[8]

We can look at another area of inquiry to discover how our hearts may affect perceptions, emotions, behaviours, and more—and may even be a 'thinking' organ in its own right. There are some fascinating stories coming from heart transplant recipients, for example as recounted in Dr Paul Pearsall's book *The Heart's Code*. The experiences of this special group of people reveal that our hearts are thinking organs in their own right complete with memories.

In one example, Pearsall tells of an 8-year-old girl who received a heart transplant from a 10-year-old girl who was murdered. After a successful operation, the 8 year old began having nightmares about the man who had killed her donor. Distressed, the girl's mother took her to see a psychiatrist, who after a couple of sessions began to think the girl might not just be having a stress response to her life-threatening health problems and the major life change of her receiving a new heart. The psychiatrist could not deny what she was being told by the child. The girl's mother, too, came to suspect that perhaps this information might be useful to the police. It took some time, but she finally overcame her resistance and called the appropriate authorities, who came and talked to the girl. Astonishingly, armed with the description of the man and other information about the murder weapon and circumstances of the crime that the little girl gave them, the police were able to find the murderer, who was eventually convicted.[9]

Dr Pearsall has amassed a library of such stories, and the only common factor is that each of the people are heart-transplant recipients. Pearsall's conclusion is that the heart somehow stores memories, and when one person's heart is placed into another person's body, some of the donor's memories become available to the recipient. Other researchers have found the same phenomenon, although not all heart transplant patients report such 'donor memories'. A more common occurrence is the recipient suddenly taking on new behaviours, opinions and habits, such as liking new foods,using odd language phrases, or shifting deep-rooted aspects of their personalities. Usually, when information about the heart donor can be tracked down, it turns out the recipient's new behaviours or preferences match those of the donor. Through the donor's heart and the energy fields it carries, the recipient may become 'imprinted' with new information.

Heart intuition or intelligence takes us to a whole new level of possibility in terms of thinking about who we are, what influences us and how we interact with the world around us. By fostering greater heart rhythm coherence, we foster better health and greater self-awareness. We can also harmonise that which is inside us with that which is outside us, bringing a greater balance to our lives. Knowing our heart is a sensory and memory organ, we can celebrate it as a new 'tool'—beyond the incredible computing power of our brain—to lift ourselves to new levels of insight,achievement, performance, contentment and creativity. The heart and brain are uniquely connected, with the heart sometimes taking the lead in processing information and emotions. Creating a coherent heartbeat-rate pattern is an effective and efficient way of accessing our higher brain functions and is a very important component of the Gamma Belief Change Technique and the Gamma Brain Technique© I will share later in this book.

Because the coherence of your heart–brain connection is so important to the science of how we repattern our subconscious minds with new empowering beliefs, let me end this chapter with an overview of the four ways the heart communicates with the brain, according to research from the discipline of neurocardiology and other areas, such as the work of the Heart Math Institute.

1. The first route of heart–brain communication is the most obvious: through the transmission of nerve impulses via the nervous system.
2. The second way is with chemicals such as hormones and neurotransmitters. It was a huge surprise to researchers to find the

heart producing and using biochemicals that they previously thought only the brain used. The heart produces such powerful hormones as atrial peptide, which reduces the stress hormone cortisol. That the heart actually produces this peptide means that, contrary to previous biological knowledge, the heart—and not just the brain—is designed to help relieve stress. The heart also produces oxytocin, which is known as the 'love hormone'. Isn't it interesting that the organ we associate so closely with love actually produces the love hormone? The heart also produces dopamine. Dopamine is produced for many reasons, one of which is to facilitate learning, especially when we are forming new habits and behaviours.

3. The third way the heart communicates with the brain is biophysically—that is, through energy fields that affect the body. For example, when the heart beats, it creates a wave of energy called a blood pressure wave. This blood pressure wave reaches the brain before the blood and changes brain activity. As the blood pressure wave changes, so does the electrical activity of the brain.

4. The fourth way, and possibly the most exciting way, is via purely energetic connections, such as electromagnetic fields. The heart is our main electrical power centre. It produces two and a half watts of electrical power, which is 40 to 60 times more wattage than is produced by the electrical activity of the brain. If you plugged a light bulb into your heart energy, it would light up. (This may explain how we could light up neon bulbs at The Monroe Institute; see Chapter 5.) Interestingly, you can record your heart beat anywhere on your body. That's because every time your heart beats, the electrical field it produces permeates every cell, forming a potential body-wide communication network. In fact your thoughts and feelings are communicated to every cell of your body via this electromagnetic superhighway. What is more, this electromagnetic field doesn't just radiate throughout your body, but actually streams from you to the outside world, in a 360-degree field that is shaped like a torus (a ring doughnut) and that radiates up to 15 feet outside your body. It is actually thought to extend much further, but our current

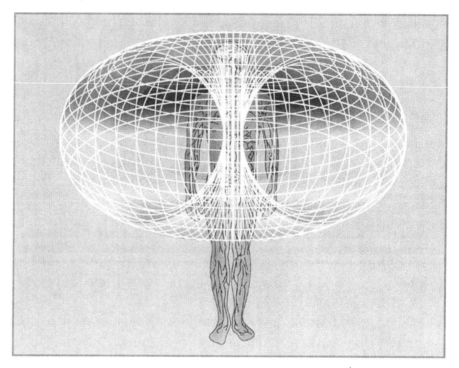

Figure 6.3   *The heart's electromagnetic field.*

measuring equipment can only confirm its extension to this distance. (See Figure 6.3.)

That our heart field extends so far outside our body may explain why we can sense 'emotional atmospheres' so easily. The frequencies of the heart actually change depending on how we feel. Our emotional state influences changes in our electromagnetic personal energy signature. Since its field is much more powerful than the brain's, it stands to reason that it is a more powerful 'detector' than the brain. This may be why you immediately sense 'something wrong' when you walk into a room, or, conversely, may immediately feel a space is 'sacred' or 'special'. We are all literally broadcasting our emotional and mental energies out into the world, and research such as that I have already talked about, and other studies, such as that by physicist William Tiller (see Chapter 8), suggests that this energy signature can be literally imprinted into the environment. We pick up these types of feeling first through our heart field, which as an information processor then sends this information to our brain, where our reasoning capacities kick in and we can decide what actions, if any, we need to take or what response is appropriate.

Aligning your heart and brain is essential for optimal mind–body performance. But there is more to know, so that you will be fully informed about how and why your beliefs are formed, processed in your mind–body, and then used to create what you call 'your life'. I devote one more chapter to fascinating research that I trust will impress you with how much knowledge you have in your mind–body and how important it is to align your subconscious with your consciousness in order to shift old belief patterns into new, more empowering ones. The information in the next chapter will bring home to you just how important it is when changing belief patterns to work through your body instead of trying to use only willpower and positive thinking.

Enter the human matrix...

Key Points

❏ The brain's ability to change is almost infinite.

❏ Activating the brain's frontal lobes and balancing the left and right hemispheres is required for effective belief and behaviour change.

❏ The heart is directly involved with processing external information and is capable of precognition.

❏ Accessing emotional states such as love, caring, gratitude, appreciation and generally feeling really good creates coherent health-promoting heart rhythms that activate the frontal cortex—the most evolved part of the brain.

❏ The heart's electromagnetic field broadcasts your emotional personal energy signature outside of the body.

7

THE HUMAN MATRIX

The cell is a machine driven by energy. It can thus be approached by studying matter, or by studying energy. In every culture and in every medical tradition before ours, healing was accomplished by moving energy.
Professor Albert Szent-Gyorgyi, Nobel Laureate in Medicine

In this chapter we bring our understanding of the human mind and body up to date with the latest science, which is tremendously empowering and beneficial for us to know.[1]

First, let's journey back a few centuries to see just how far we have come. For centuries scientists have been searching for the magic formula that controls life. In the sixteenth century Isaac Newton, physicist and mathematician, saw the universe as a great big machine made of physical parts that was predictable and mechanistic. He measured the mass, acceleration and direction of the earth, moon, sun and planets. He believed you could understand the nature of the universe by measuring the physical properties alone. This led to a belief in 'materialism', which says that physical matter is the only or fundamental reality. There was not the knowledge or awareness in Newton's day to study, measure and understand the invisible information and energy fields we know and use today. Physics is the parent science and leads the way for the rest of our sciences. As the universe was seen as a physical machine made out of physical parts, the rest of the sciences followed suit and focused on studying its purely physical properties. If we lived in a purely physical universe, then to understand what controls our human lives we would look for physical things within us. What is it that controls our lives and makes us the way we are?

In 1859 Charles Darwin wrote in his book *On the Origin of Species* that a person's traits were passed from parents to their children. He suggested that something physical was passed from the parent to the child and these 'hereditary traits' controlled the characteristics of an individual's life. From this 'belief' scientists set off on a mission to find what this physical mechanism was that controlled our lives. What controls our strengths, our intellectual, artistic and physical abilities and what determines our weaknesses such as cancer, cardiovascular disease or depression? As Dr Bruce Lipton explains in his book *The Biology of Belief*,

> *That bit of insight set scientists off on a frenzied attempt to dissect life down to its molecular nuts and bolts, for they thought that within the structure of the human cells was to be found the heredity mechanism that controls life.*

1953 Headline News: 'Secret of Life Discovered'

One hundred years on from Darwin in 1953, James Watson and Francis Crick hypothesised that the DNA molecule in each of our cells, containing the genes, was this governing mechanism that controlled the potential of our lives. Think of the DNA molecule in our cells as a vast cookbook full of recipes. The recipes are the genes. To read the recipes/genes you need a cook. Bring in the cook, the RNA molecule. The cook/RNA molecule reads the recipes/genes and forms the ingredients together. The ingredients are proteins and the proteins make our cells. Our human bodies are made of a community of approximately 50 to 100 trillion cells.

From Watson and Crick's hypothesis the 'central dogma' of biology was born. It was said that it was our genes that controlled our lives. If you got a 'fat gene' or a 'happy gene', a 'depressed gene' or an 'alcoholic gene', 'a homosexual gene' or a 'genius gene', then that is what you would become. Your strengths, weaknesses, abilities and potentials were all believed to be pre-programmed by the genes. Great if you got a good set, but pretty bleak if you got a bad set. Genes were seen as king of the castle and the search for what controlled life was over. This was known as 'genetic determinism'. Now here's the kicker, this was never ever a scientific fact, but a hypothesis that became an unquestioned belief.

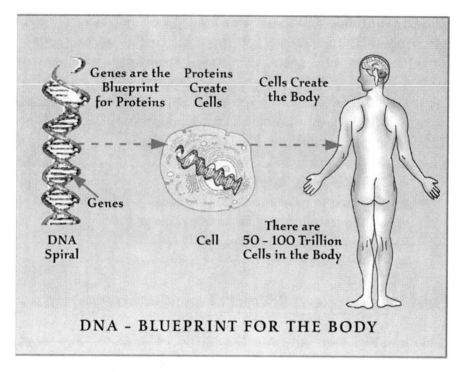

Figure 7.1   The deterministic genetic program for the human body.

This is one of the most disempowering beliefs there is. It leads us to the belief that we are pre-programmed, fixed, physical machines that were 'just born that way'. It can lead to a subconscious victim mentality with no understanding that we are in charge of our own destiny and have massive potential to change. There is no room here for the power of the mind.

Fortunately, the current understanding at the leading edge of science shows us a completely different picture of how life works. We now understand that the environment, and specifically our beliefs about the environment, directly control the activity of our DNA and genes. This is known as epigenetic control: 'epi' meaning above; control above the genes. Our beliefs, attitudes and overall mindset to life are the all-governing factors in what happens in our body and inevitably our life. Thankfully, reductionist, deterministic science is losing steam in the sciences. As Dr Bruce Lipton continues:

We are living in exciting times, for science is in the process of shattering old myths and rewriting a fundamental belief of human civilisation. The belief that we are frail biochemical machines controlled by genes is giving way to an understanding that we are powerful creators of our lives and the world in which we live.

Our genes have little if anything to do with our traits, personality, characteristics, abilities and potential. In the nature versus nurture debate, nurture is the king. Our early programming and the way we update and program our minds are the determining factors in the quality and success of our lives.

In 2008 pop singer Madonna adopted a baby from a peasant family in Malawi, Africa. Just imagine the difference to this baby's life now, living in the luxurious West with all the best care, nutrition and education, compared to a peasant's village life where her parents could not read or write and resources were very scarce. The abilities and outcome to this child's life are not controlled by the genes of the parents but by nurture and environmental programming. As Dr Carl Ratner from the Institute for Cultural Research and Education, Trinidad, California says:

Genes may directly determine simple physical characteristics such as eye colour. However they do not directly determine psychological phenomena.[2]

It's not only our personalities that are shaped by our environment and beliefs, our bodies and health are too. Dr Andrew Weil, professor and pioneer of alternative and complementary medicine, reports that 'a study of nearly 1,000 older adults followed for nine years concluded that people with high levels of optimism had a 23% lower risk of death from cardiovascular disease and a 55% lower risk of death from other causes compared to their pessimistic peers'.[3] Their physiology was not slavishly following the orders of their genes, but was deeply influenced by their state of mind and personality traits. Dr Lipton concurs, saying,

There are some genetic defects called birth defects, but over 95% of the people on this planet arrived into this world with a healthy set of genes. It has also been shown that over 95% of cancer has no genetic linkage. It is the individual's experience of life based on their perceptions. If you change the beliefs and perceptions, you can change the presence of the cancer.[4]

The bottom line is that our destiny does not lie in our genes, but in our beliefs, and that is ultra powerful.

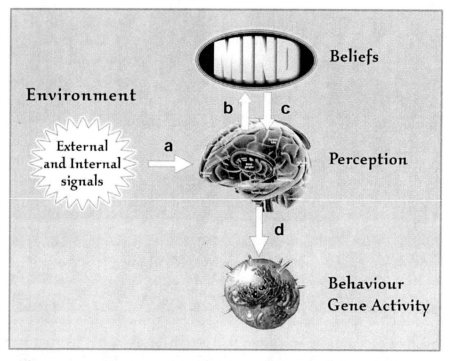

Figure 7.2   *Our beliefs control our perceptions of the environment, which then influence the functions of our cells and even of our DNA. (Image used with the kind permission of Dr Bruce Lipton.)*

Quantum Physics Changed Everything

In the 1920s, science underwent a startling transformation with the rise of quantum physics. Physicists developed technology that could go beyond the level of solid material things to measure the very tiny realms of nature at the level of atoms and smaller particles like electrons and protons. It also studies energy fields and forces at the most fundamental levels of the universe. When reductionist scientists began taking apart cells, molecule by molecule, atom by atom, to study them, they discovered that 'matter' dissolves into nothingness, for the atoms that make up matter—including your body, a chair, a steel bar, the food you eat—are 99.9999% empty space. But this nothingness is itself not so empty. It is full of energy and information. In fact, these invisible vibrating fields of energy and information are actually what create the physical world.[5]

You are familiar with some of these 'invisible' energy and information fields. The gravitational field keeps you firmly on the earth, and it gives things 'weight'. It keeps the moon circling the earth, and the earth and other planets circling the sun, instead of flying into outer space. It causes the ocean to have tides. Think, too, of the magnetic field. Put iron filings near the end of a magnet, and they arrange themselves in an orderly way, forming along the curvature of the magnetic field. We live in a sea of radio waves that come from thousands of radio and television stations, mobile phone and internet networks. You may have seen or heard of soprano singers whose vocal energy field can cause a glass goblet to explode. When the singer's voice vibrates 'in resonance' with the vibrations of the glass, the goblet can shatter.

The fields I have just talked about have a presence that we can easily feel or infer in the macro world of matter. Quantum energy and information fields underlie the way your body and mind work, and they have real influence in your life, as we will now explore.[6]

Your Body's Warp-Speed Matrix Communication System

Your body produces its own fields of energy and information. In fact, it has two communication systems, a chemical-signalling system and an electromagnetic information signalling system. It is the latter that is the predominant vehicle for programming the mind and integrating new belief systems. Your perceptions of life from your five physical senses and heart intuitions are sent to your brain, which directs cascades of chemicals, enzymes and hormones around your body via your autonomic nervous system to perform various functions, maintain balance and keep your body safe. As you saw in the last chapter, your heart radiates your emotions in a 360-degree electromagnetic field outside of your body and into the environment. Electromagnetic fields affect every cell of your body, and they are integral to the structure and form of all material systems, from atoms to galaxies.

The electromagnetic system of the body is commonly referred to as the 'living matrix', a phrase coined by biophysicist Dr James Oschman. I will talk more about this system later in this chapter, but for now the important point is that this matrix runs on waves of electromagnetic energy and information. The nervous system using chemicals as its information messengers is a bit like an old telephone exchange and the electromagnetic system is more like a fibre-optic cable system that sends information at vastly higher speeds to a more comprehensive network. (A single fibre-optic telephone cable thinner than a human hair can carry 200,000 conversations simultaneously.) Both systems activate your body's cells so that they can properly perform their required functions. The chemical messengers travel just under a centimetre a second, whereas the information signals of the electromagnetic system would have travelled three-quarters of the way to the moon in that time.[7]

Here's a way to think concretely about these two signalling systems in your body. A friend of mine recently purchased a new Aston Martin car. It is very swish, and he can start it in two different ways. He can put the key in the ignition and turn the key to start it up the mechanical way, which equates with the chemical signalling in your body, or he can press a button on a key fob from some distance away, which sends a signal to the car's computer system and the engine starts. This equates with the electromagnetic matrix system of your body.

In the 1970s, Oxford biophysicist C.W.F. McClare calculated that electromagnetic frequencies are a hundred times more efficient than chemical signals such as hormones, pharmaceutical drugs and neurotransmitters in relaying information within biological systems.[8] But exactly how do these electromagnetic signals move through your body matrix?

Your organs and muscular system are encased with a kind of connective tissue called fascia. (See Figure 7.3.) This connective tissue fascia, when taken as a whole, is the largest organ of your body. The molecules in this connective tissue network are structured in a highly regular parallel fashion. Molecules that have this type of structure are called 'crystals'. We tend to think of crystals as hard things like diamonds or quartz, and we do not think of our bodies as having crystalline properties, but they actually do.

When looked at under a microscope, these fascia structures reveal themselves to be soft, flexible liquid crystals, and we know from physics that crystalline structures are remarkable receivers of energy and information. Many researchers are exploring how this crystalline system sends and receives messages, and what its functions are in the body.

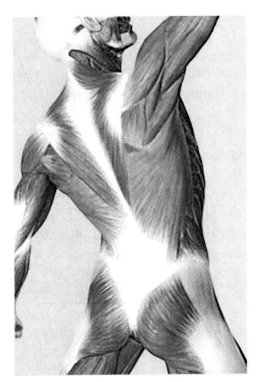

Figure 7.3   The Fascia System of the Body.

Harvard researcher Dr Donald Ingber provided some of the first scientific evidence of the existence of the structure and its make-up. In his article 'The architecture of life', published in *Scientific American* in 1998, he reported that all life forms—from viruses to vertebrates—have the same underlying structure at the molecular level. He calls this structure the 'tensegrity matrix'. (It is the same system that I refer to using Dr Oschman's term, the living matrix.) This is a crystalline structure that connects all parts of the body, making for a system-wide channel of communication. The information it carries is received not only from your cells, hormones and other biochemical substances, but also from your mind—your emotions, thoughts, perceptions and beliefs. It's why we can say that the mind–body can be thought of not as two separate but connected systems, but as one seamless system.

As we have seen, our beliefs and perceptions are the basis for our thoughts and feelings. Our thoughts and feelings are waves of electromagnetic energy and information that permeate each and every cell in our mind–body system via this connective tissue crystalline matrix. Dr Lipton explains,

> *Every cell is a programmable chip, and the nucleus of the cell is the hard disk with programs. But, like a computer, it is the programmer that controls the disk, not the disk that controls the programmer.*[9]

We are the programmers. These signals of our bodies work in a feedback loop with our brains, and both consciously and subconsciously govern our choices. Our choices, of course, drastically influence the condition of our lives. (See Figure 7.4.) The implications are immense. As Dr Herbert Benson, pioneer of mind–body medicine, has said, after decades of research at Harvard Medical School and other places,

> *Even though science cannot measure most of the myriads of interactions entertained in the brain, we should not ignore compelling brain research that demonstrates that beliefs manifest themselves throughout our bodies.*[10]

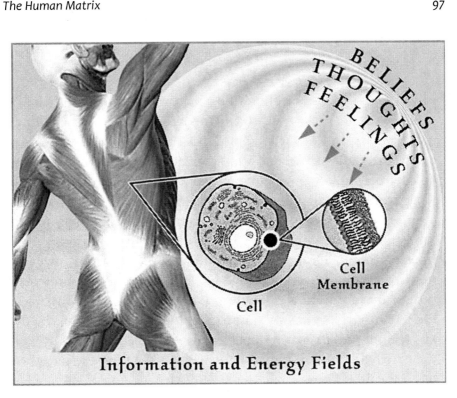

Figure 7.4   The living matrix is a systems-wide communication network, linking our thoughts, emotions, and beliefs with our body, and vice versa.

The living matrix means that quite literally what we think and feel in large measure is what we become, as each of our 50 to 100 trillion cells receives and sends information at lightning speed throughout our mind–body, communicating with all other cells like a vast inner computer network. As esteemed physics Professor John Hagelin explains succinctly:

> *It is important to recognise that our body is really the product of our thoughts, we are beginning to understand in medical science the degree to which the nature of our thoughts and emotions actually determine the physical substance and structure and function of our bodies.*[11]

Energy Fields and the Human Body

For more than 5000 years, eastern medical systems have recognised the reality that the human body uses energy fields to function. The most well-formulated theory is of the Chinese meridian system. These are vessels or channels of energy that circulate throughout the body carrying and regulating vital energy. They are accessed through acupuncture points at the skin level. The western medical establishment finally caught up with the Chinese in 1995, as the existence of energy channels running in the body exactly where the Chinese plotted them was confirmed by experiment. Dr Pierre de Vernejoul and his team injected a non-toxic radioactive tracer dye into the legs of his volunteers at the commonly used acupuncture points of the meridian system. He then used gamma camera imaging to trace the flow of the dye. His team found that the radioactive dye travelled specifically along the clearly defined meridian network that the Chinese have been using for thousands of years. When the dye was injected elsewhere in the body, randomly and not at known acupuncture points, it did not move along any specific pathway. This work began a period of more intensive study by other researchers of the meridian system, which Ted Kaptchuk, doctor of traditional Chinese medicine, described as 'an invisible network that links together all the relevant substances and organs' of the body.[12]

In another scientific validation of the acupuncture meridians, professor of physics Zang-Hee Cho, from the University of California, Irvine, discovered that pressure on the vision-related acupuncture points on the outside of the foot almost instantaneously activates the visual cortex in the brain, as measured by a functional brain scan.[13] (See Figure 7.5.) In fact, acupuncture needling these specific points on the foot had the same impact on the brain as shining a torch light into the participant's eyes. The speed of this energy transfer is far too fast for it to be conducted by nerve impulses.[14] Many studies have shown that the meridian pathways are low-resistance pathways for the flow of electricity.[15] As Dr James Oschman concludes,

The meridians then are simply the main channels or transmission lines in the continuous molecular fabric of the body.[16]

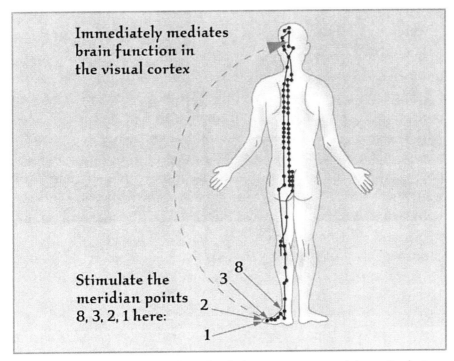

Figure 7.5 *Research showed that stimulating acupuncture points on the foot that were said by the Chinese to stimulate the eyes and vision did indeed stimulate the visual cortex, even though there is no known mechanism in traditional medicine or biology to explain this cause–effect phenomenon.*

Research at Harvard Medical School by Dr Bruce Rosen showed that needling an acupuncture point on the hand known as Large Intestine 4, which is believed to help ease pain, caused immediate blood-flow changes to the amygdala and related areas of the brain that correlate with pain, mood and cravings. The reduction in blood flow to these areas lead to an increase in endorphins, the brain's natural pain-relieving pleasure chemicals.[17] Other research showed that activating specific acupuncture points correlated with enhanced serotonin secretion. Serotonin is our feel-good chemical. This research and other studies have shown without a doubt that activating particular acupuncture points correlates to specific effects in precise areas of the brain. Even applying pressure to acupuncture points, called acupressure, instead of inserting needles, produces very effective results.

The benefits of such non-invasive techniques can be enormous. For example, acupuncture and acupressure can calm deep brain structures, such as the limbic system. When the limbic system is activated, your nervous system initiates a body-wide fight-or-flight response, which induces stress and causes your prefrontal cortex, one of your higher thought centres, to go 'offline' temporarily. So knowing some acupressure points can be a helpful response to dilute stress. However, for our purposes, the noteworthy point is that for optimal mind–body coherence, you want to remove as many of these stressors from your subconscious memory banks as possible. Knowing some acupressure points and other techniques for coherence in your body's energetic and physical systems can help you easily reduce the impact of negative and persistent emotional patterns that may have been causing stress on your nervous system for years, limiting your potential.

You do not need to be an acupuncturist to benefit from using your meridian system to enhance your health and well-being. Applying pressure with your fingers to the proper points is all that it takes to produce excellent results. Psychological issues, fears, anxieties and other stressors create a disturbance in the body's electrical systems and some of the meridians can 'seize up' like a kink in a garden hose. Tapping, holding or massaging the acupuncture points stimulates the receptors on your skin. These receptors respond to mechanical forces, such as tapping, by transferring signals to the respective nerve centres of the brain. If you recall an emotional problem and begin tapping the appropriate acupuncture point, signals are sent to your brain, and the pathways associated with this emotional problem are disrupted, the neurochemical endorphins (endorphins are 27 times more powerful than morphine) are released and the energy is diffused and re-imprinted so that the pathways will not be activated in the same way again. This is an easy and effective way to recondition your subconscious and improve your capacity for positive change, so why not give it a try? Overleaf is a meridian system-tapping technique to relieve stress that is correlated to unresourceful emotions. (You can see a video demonstration of this technique by going to www.ChrisWaltonUK.com – videos tab.)

The Emotional Balance Technique©

❏ Think of an issue, person, event or situation that causes stress or an emotional reaction. It should be something that provokes an emotional charge in your nervous system, a reaction and feeling that you would rather not have.

❏ Rate the charge you get from the issue on a scale of one to ten, with ten being a highly charged feeling and one being not really an issue.

❏ To eliminate the emotional and psychological stress from an issue or problem, tap the ten meridian points shown on page 102/103. Tap each point nine times. Under the description of the meridian tapping points are the related emotions.

❏ Continue to think of and feel the effects of the issue as you tap the points. Say out loud or quietly to yourself what the issue is you are releasing, such as 'angry with my boss', which you would repeat through the entire sequence of tapping.

❏ The tapping pressure is quite gentle, (you do not need to be like a woodpecker). Be aware of the physical pressure you use and also aim to increase your awareness to feel the energetic transfer. The more you practise this the more you will be able to feel the energy moving. Apart from point 1, tap the points using all four fingers and thumb, in the following order:

1. **Sides of the hands together.** (Small intestine meridian—removes self-doubt, feelings of low self-esteem and improves self-confidence.)

2. **Crown suture, a straight line from the crown of your head to your forehead.** (You do not need to bend your head down, that is for demonstration purposes only. Many meridians meet at the top of the head—removes self-critical thinking and lack of focus.)

3. **Eyebrows.** (Bladder meridian—removes trauma, hurt, sadness, frustration, impatience; improves inner peace and calm.)

4. **Temples.** (Gall bladder meridian—removes rage, anger, resentment, fear of change; improves clarity and compassion.)

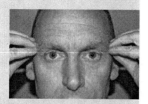

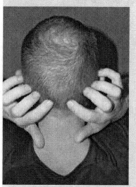

5. **Back of the head, where the top of the neck joins the skull.** (Several meridians run over the head—this point helps remove all of the above emotions.)

6. **Side of lips to side of eyes—index finger on edge of eye, little finger to corner of mouth.**

(Stomach and small intestine meridian—removes fear, anxiety, emptiness, worry, nervousness, loneliness and disappointment, helps improve calmness, contentment and feeling safe.)

7. **Under nose.** (Governing meridian—removes embarrassment, powerlessness, shame, guilt, grief, fear of ridicule; helps improve self-acceptance, personal power and compassion for self and others.)

8. **Under bottom lip.** (Central meridian—removes confusion, uncertainty, shame, embarrassment; helps improve clarity, certainty and confidence.)

9. **Four inches under the armpits—tap both sides.** (Spleen meridian—removes guilt, worry, obsessing, hopelessness, insecurity; helps improve clarity, confidence and relaxation.)

10. **Collarbone/thymus point, approx. two inches down from your sternal notch.** (Kidney meridian—removes indecision, feeling stuck, worry, fear; helps improve confidence and clarity to move forward.)

When you have finished the tapping procedure, check in emotionally and rate your stress about the issue again, using the same scale of one to ten.

People who use this meridian-tapping technique report dramatically reduced stress and emotional charge around the issue, allowing them to move forward and make decisions with clarity and wisdom.

There may be several aspects to an issue. For example, one of my coaching clients was angry about how she was being treated by her boss. We removed the anger from her mind–body, then she began to feel frustration that she was not treated fairly; she then moved to feeling anxious and then demotivated and lethargic about her work in general. After about five rounds of tapping the ten acu points, she was free of these emotions and could not get them back. You keep going until you have worked through all the issues that you feel are draining your emotional energy and throwing your system off balance. This is very powerful and takes just minutes.

Using this simple but effective technique is a safe and free way to maintain or increase your emotional and mental health. It also increases your internal coherence, aligning mind and body, and, by doing so, helps to improve your performance in just about every area of your life. On a physical level, you are removing stress from your nervous system, which is freeing up energy for you to do more. On an emotional level, this new reservoir of energy can help you better express who you are and so help you better utilise your gifts and talents.

These ten acupuncture points rapidly enhance immune system function and power up the entire meridian network, increasing harmony and coherence throughout every cell of the mind–body system.

* * *

So far in this book, I have educated you about how beliefs affect every aspect of your mind and body. Your conscious and subconscious intentions, fuelled by your desires, drive energy through your meridian system, which in turn influences the health of all your organs, neural systems and cells. This revitalisation of your physical body can help make you feel more alive. In addition, your emotions radiate outwards into the world, mostly via your heart's electromagnetic field. Let's examine one last aspect of your energy system before we move on, the energy field of your thoughts.

One of the ways scientists measure the neural activity of the brain is by using an electroencephalograph (EEG) (see Figure 7.6). As nerve cells fire in the brain, they create different kinds of electrical patterns, and the EEG can detect and report on these patterns. The most common brain-wave patterns are beta, alpha, theta and delta waves, which I talked about in Chapter 3.

With electrical currents also come magnetic currents, and your brain produces a magnetic field that can be detected outside

Figure 7.6 *Electroencephalography uses electrodes carefully placed on the skull to detect the many kinds of electrical patterns created by the cellular and other functions of your brain. These patterns are classified into the different kinds of brain waves.*

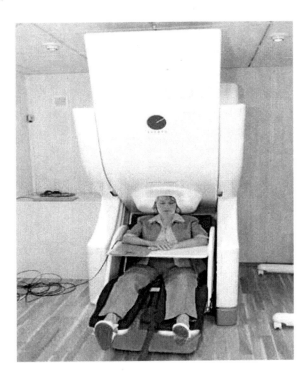

Figure 7.7 *The SQUID technology detects and measures magnetic fields streaming from your brain into the space surrounding your head.*

of your skull in the space surrounding you. This magnetic field can be detected and measured by a technology called magneto-encephalography (MEG) and, more specifically, by a leading-edge 'quantum technology' called the Super Quantum Induction Device, or SQUID for short (see Figure 7.7). The SQUID measures the field not at the scalp, but out in the space surrounding the head. Basically, it is detecting the electromagnetic activity of your brain—in effect, your personal energy signature of your thoughts which are broadcast into your environment, 24 hours a day, every day of your life.

You are literally submersed in a vibrational information field of your own thoughts and emotions, and because electromagnetic fields propagate outwards to infinity, your personal energy field is interconnected with the emotional and thought fields of every other person on earth.

Inevitably our lives are the way they are because our belief, thought and emotion fields have created them this way. This is a really important concept to get your head around: your thought and emotion fields form and structure the quantum waves and particles, which in turn form the atoms, molecules, cells, body and so on. This is great news! Change your vibration via your beliefs and perceptions and your world literally starts to vibrate at a different frequency, bringing new things into manifestation. As you vibrate at new levels that support your growth and happiness, you attract similar people, events and experiences into your life. Good times ahead!

Where does your emotion/thought field go? Does it dissipate after a while into the ether, like breath on a misty morning, or does it stay around in some sort of universal memory field for ever? How does your emotion/thought field interact with the fields of others? Does this global mind energy field really exist, and if so, what consequence does it have for your life and for the state of the world? Let's journey a bit further along the road of inquiry to discover even more reasons why each and every one of us stands to benefit when we update our belief systems and turn self-sabotaging thoughts into self-supporting ones. You've been patient as I have led you through the science supporting the reality of energy fields in your body and your brain. You've gained a deeper understanding of the science supporting the Gamma Belief-Change Technique I will teach you and why it will be of tremendous benefit to you—and to the world. In the next chapter, we will look at the fascinating fact that we are part of a global mind, and you will see that when you expand and increase your own potential and abilities you help others to do so too.

Key Points

❑ Invisible energy and information fields form the physical matter of life.

❑ Genes do not shape your personality or control your potential.

❑ Your beliefs are broadcast to every cell of your body almost instantaneously through the matrix system.

❑ The electromagnetic energy of your thoughts is broadcast out of your skull into the world 24 hours a day.

8

THE GLOBAL INTERCONNECTED MIND

If you follow where our research is going in our lab and other labs, it leads us to the conclusion that we are all interconnected through our consciousness and energy; therefore, we need to become conscious of this and transform our consciousness so we can take more responsibility for the effects that we are having.
Gary Schwartz, Professor of Psychology, Neurology, Psychiatry, Medicine and Surgery

We have moved from the belief in the universe being a great big clockwork machine, with human beings as purely physical individual machines made of physical parts, to a quantum interconnected universe full of energy and information, and where human beings radiate their emotional and mental energy and information out into the world 24 hours a day. Once scientists were able to detect and explore the subatomic world—the realm of energy and information fields—the world not only saw the rise of a new scientific paradigm, but was profoundly changed across the board. This new understanding of how nature works will have the largest effect on human civilisation since we realised that the earth revolves around the sun.

Many scientists, including the renowned psychologist Carl Jung, posit that human beings have both an individual mind and a collective mind. According to Jung, this collective mind, which he called the 'collective unconscious', is a kind of universal psychic repository of our human history—including all of the world's cultural myths, legends, symbols and human reactions—that we access continually, expressing itself as our belief system through archetypes (like God as an old man with a white beard, for example), culture and religion.[1] He is not alone: thinkers and scientists past and present offer the same insight. Two thousand years ago, Patanjali, the Hindu philosopher and Sanskrit writer of the Yoga sutras, taught that a 'non-local universal mind' was accessible as a sort of repository of information—called the Akashic records—and it imprints all the information in the world, past and present. It even contains information about the future. Some modern scientists and philosophers offer similar opinions. For example, Professor Ervin Laszlo, esteemed philosopher and one of the fathers of systems theory, writes in his best-selling book *Science and the Akashic Field*,

> *Recent discoveries in physics show this Akashic field is real. This field consists of a sea of fluctuating energies and information from which all things arise, from atoms and galaxies, stars and planets, living beings and even consciousness. This field is a memory bank of the entire universe from day one to now. It holds the record of all that ever happened on earth and in the cosmos and relates it to all that is yet to happen.*[2]

Laszlo's 'A-field', as he calls it, is not some metaphysical or spiritual mind field, but a real field predicted by quantum theory called the zero-point field.

All of our thoughts, feelings and actions—from the beginning of human history and extending into all of our possible futures—are energy and information fields. Everything in this world has a vibration, from subatomic energy and information fields to atoms, molecules, cells, tissues, organs, to us as human beings with a physical body.

We are literally first and foremost vibrational beings of energy and information encompassed in larger fields of energy (see Figure 8.1). Our behaviours, then, are directed and determined not only by our nervous system and the physical and chemical processes that go on within our bodies, but also by the organising activity of the fields of energy and information that underlie and drive these chemical and physical processes. That we are energy beings has profound implications, because it means that we are connected to all other energy fields, including those of other human beings. As Albert Einstein said so eloquently:

> *A human being is a part of a whole, called by us the universe, a part limited in time and space. He experiences himself, his thoughts and feelings, as something separated from the rest, a kind of optical delusion of his consciousness. This delusion is a kind of prison for us, restricting us to our personal desires and to affection for a few persons nearest to us. Our task must be to free ourselves from this prison by widening our circle of compassion to embrace all living creatures and the whole of nature in its beauty.[3]*

The new physics shows us that the universe is not a collection of discrete objects, but a holistic, integrative connected realm. Because everything in the universe is interdependent, at some level everything influences everything else. Although Figure 8.1 appears to show the realms of the universe as hierarchical, each realm is actually embedded in and even emerges from the level below it. All are connected at the deepest levels of reality. Each and every one of us is part of an interconnected 'global mind' at a subconscious level. Let's look at how science is offering substantial new evidence to support this view.

The Evidence for Our Interconnectedness

In quantum physics there are two phenomena that reveal the interconnectedness of everything in the universe. These are entanglement and non-locality. These two concepts are majorly important for us to know, as when we apply these principles to our lives a deep personal transformation can take place.

We are all made of subatomic particles and waves, as is everything in the universe. So where is the boundary between the two worlds: the subatomic world of energy and information and our physical day-to-day world? That question is a deep one, and it occupies some of the best philosophic and scientific minds in the world. Many of these theoreticians have come to the conclusion that there is no boundary. That the universe is one great entangled web of energy and information—that everything must be inter-

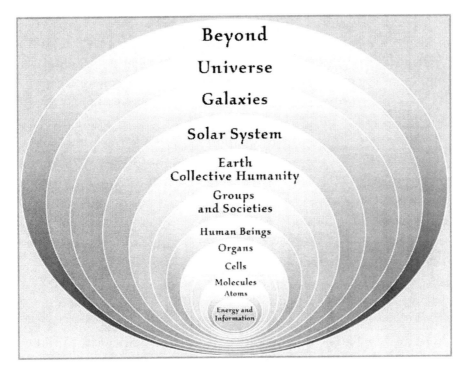

Beyond

Universe

Galaxies

Solar System

Earth
Collective Humanity

Groups
and Societies

Human Beings

Organs

Cells

Molecules

Atoms

Energy and
Information

Figure 8.1   The universe can be categorised into discrete realms, but science is showing that each realm emerges and is structured from the one below it.

connected at some deep level of reality. At the deepest level, we are interconnected with each other and with everything in the universe. In fact, some physicists, such as Professor Amit Goswami, believe the universe can be thought of as self-aware and conscious, because we, as conscious beings, create it with our thoughts, feelings and actions.[4]

The quantum evidence for interconnectedness is only 'weird' from a Newtonian 'clockwork machine' perspective. It makes sense if everything is connected via energy and information. So let's turn now from theoretical science to hard, meaningful-to-us evidence, where the experiments are being done that show our energetic connections. In one of the most persuasive experiments, subtle connections appeared to link two people such that their effect could be measured physically. Here's how the experiment went.

Two people are put in separate rooms that are shielded from any electromagnetic energy, are sound-proofed and are otherwise protected from any kind of known force, field or signal. Both are hooked up to brain-monitoring equipment, such that they can be continually monitored individually. A light is flashed randomly in the eyes of one of the subjects, which causes effects in his brain. The equipment measures the expected changes in the visual area and other areas of his brain when it is stimulated by the light flashing. Nothing is out of the ordinary here. What is astounding, however, is that the brain-monitoring equipment for the other subject picks up exactly the same brain stimulation at the time of the light flashing, even though no light is flashing in her eyes. Somehow, what happens to one of the pair affects the physical system of the other, even though they are far apart in separate rooms that are both shielded against signal penetration.

Dr Dean Radin, senior scientist at the Institute of Noetic Sciences, who conducts some of the most rigorous studies exploring what is commonly referred to as the 'paranormal', especially as it relates to entanglement between human beings, is extremely vocal about what these kinds of experiments tell us—that we are entangled beings and what happens to one of us may influence others, even if we are not consciously aware of the influence—and also about how the scientific establishment refuses to take these studies seriously, even though they meet the 'gold standard' in terms of experimental methodology. He believes this evidence, which has been amassing for decades, is so important that it should be the biggest news of the day, as it totally changes how we think of ourselves and our place in the world. He says, with his characteristic humour,

> *This discovery is so shocking that it is virtually guaranteed no one would hear about it, despite it being published in a medical journal. This is worse than missing a story about aliens landing on the White House lawn. It's more like spotting an alien shopping in the frozen food section of the local grocery store and no one caring.*[5]

In one of the studies with human subjects, done in Mexico by Jacobo Grinberg-Zylberaum and Julieta Ramos, another form of entanglement came to light unexpectedly. Pairs of volunteers in separate rooms were asked to 'tune in' to each other's presence at specific, but randomly selected, times. During the time they were focusing (which means they simply directed their thoughts and attention to the other person in any way that felt comfortable to them), their brain waves, as measured on an EEG, became synchronised, whereas during the non-focus times they were not synchronised. Additional study revealed that the best synchronisation results were attained by those experimental pairs who displayed the most highly coherent natural brain-wave rhythms (that is, their baseline measure for coherence).[6] In other words, coherence had a greater effect on matter, in this case another person's brain.

In an interesting study carried out at the University of Montana, researchers studied entanglement between 'bonded pairs', which means two people with strong emotional connections (in this case, it was with husbands and wives). Each pair was separated in different rooms, and the wives had their baseline physiological responses measured via their galvanic skin responses. Some of the husbands were asked to plunge their bare feet into ice-cold water, whereas the other husbands were instructed to just sit quietly, serving as a control group. The electrical activity of the skin of the wives whose husbands plunged their feet into the ice showed an increase in arousal simultaneously with their husbands' experiences of the shock of the cold water. The change occurred even though consciously the wives knew nothing of what was happening to their husbands. The women whose husbands were just sitting quietly showed no such arousal response.

The evidence is clear. We are much more connected—at a physical level—than we ever thought. Our thoughts, beliefs, emotions—conscious and subconscious—can both influence the world of matter and respond to changes in the world (especially if the connection is through people with whom we have a close emotional bond). The truth is that we are all made of particles and waves, so it is not too much of a stretch to understand that at some deep, largely subconscious level, we are entangled. As Radin says,

> *Physicists have even speculated that entanglement extends to everything in the universe, because as far as we know, all energy and all matter emerged out of a single, primordial Big Bang. And thus everything came out of the chute already entangled... Such proposals suggest that despite everyday appearances, we might be living within a holistic, deeply interconnected reality.*[7]

It reminds me of the magical words of Master Yoda, from the *Star Wars* movie, when he says,

> *For my ally is the force, and a powerful ally it is. Life creates it, makes it grow. Its energy surrounds us and binds us. Luminous beings are we, not this crude matter. You must feel the force around you; here, between you, me, the tree, the rock, everywhere—yes.*[8]

You, too, may have experienced the phenomenon of entangled minds, a phenomenon that in popular terms is called a 'psychic connection'. You may have thought of someone you haven't seen or heard from for a long time, only to run into or receive a phone call from that person. Or you may have a particular friend or a spouse with whom you find yourself 'on the same wavelength'. You two may complete each other's sentences, or find you are thinking of the same subject, and so on. If we heighten our awareness, we will find that we all experience these kinds of synchronicities.

Biologist Rupert Sheldrake has amassed a database of more than 4500 cases of entanglement that can only be explained as occurring by what is commonly called 'extrasensory perception'.[9] By extrasensory perception he doesn't mean some special gift that only some people have, but an innate ability we all have to know, respond and influence things with other than the five known senses. His work and the work of so many other researchers is revealing that extrasensory perception is not a matter of belief—it appears to be the way nature functions.

Let me tell you about another type of study that is revealing entanglement. It involves the study of identical twins, who because they share the same DNA, are generally thought to be more 'connected' than non-twins. Here is one amazing story that is a hallmark study of 'coincidences', the word sceptics use for what may be entanglement. Twin boys were separated at birth because they were given up for adoption. So they were raised separately and never knew each other, nor did their adoptive parents have any contact. However, both couples named their adoptive son Jim. When they grew up, both Jims married a woman named Betty, then they both got divorced. Both eventually remarried—to a woman called Linda. Both became firemen. Both liked to build things and considered carpentry their main hobby. Each of them had a basement carpentry workshop, and each built a circular white bench around a tree in his back garden. Each had one son, both named James Alan. Both had a dog and gave their dog the same name— Toy. When their physiological state was measured, they had the same blood pressure, weight, pulse and sleep pattern. Their sports preferences were also almost identical, as both disliked baseball and liked stock car racing. They both owned Chevrolet cars. They both chain smoked. They both drank Miller Lite beer. When they took their families on holiday, they both went to their favourite place— the same beach in Florida.[10]

I've experienced or witnessed a couple of amazing occurrences of entanglement myself. Let me share a few with you. This is not a phenomenon that happens only to other people. It's common, and you only have to pay attention to start accumulating examples from your own life.

We Were Only Talking about You Yesterday

In 2007, I was living in Berkshire in England. I decided to move to London. In the process of gathering together all my possessions for shipment, I had to go to my mother's house in Staffordshire, quite a way away, to get some books I had stored there. The problem was that there were a lot of books—too many to fit into my car. I didn't want to make more than one trip from Staffordshire to London, as it was a journey of about two and a half hours one way. Plus, it was the weekend, I had work commitments on the following Monday and I didn't want to give up my whole weekend ferrying books. To accomplish my goal in one trip, I decided to hire a van in London, so I could just drop it off there and go to my new flat, unload and conveniently return the van. I could find one for hire easily enough, but none of the businesses would let me return the van on a Sunday, as they were all closed that day. They told me I had to drop the van off on Monday, which I couldn't do because of work. After many calls, still no joy. I decided I would just have to make several trips in my car, spend ten hours doing it, and effectively write off the weekend to this boring chore.

I drove to my mother's on Saturday morning, and after packing my car with the first load of books, and having a quick cup of tea with her, I decided to stop off and have a quick visit to my sister and nephews, who live close by. While there, I explained to them what I was doing, complaining about what a pain it was. My older nephew, James, said, 'Why don't you try and get a van here?'

'No,' I said, 'none of them will be open Sunday so I can't drop off the van then.' But James wouldn't be deterred. 'This isn't London,' he said. 'It's worth a try.'

I finally agreed. Even though Staffordshire was a long way from London, it would mean only one van trip instead of several car trips. We searched the internet on his computer for nearby van rental companies and found one. I gave them a call and explained my situation. 'Sorry,' the person on the line said. 'We're closed on Sundays.'

Arrrrrghhh! I could feel myself tense up as I thought of the multiple trips and ten hours of driving ahead of me. Maybe it was desperation, or maybe intuition, but on the spur of the moment I said, 'Is there any way you can help me out?'

'Hang on a minute,' said the guy on the other end of the phone. He put me on hold and when he came back on the line, he said, 'Okay. Collect the van today and I'll give you my mobile number. You can call me on Sunday when you get back here, and I'll meet you to check the van over and sign it in.'

Wow! What a helpful guy. I was delighted. 'Thanks,' I said, and quickly went off to collect the van before he changed his mind.

When I walked into the van-hire place, there was a man sitting on a sofa next to the reception counter, and I vaguely recognised him. Another man was behind the counter, and I vaguely recognised him as well. I handed over my driving licence to the man behind the counter, when the guy on the couch spoke, saying my name in a questioning voice: 'Chris Walton?' I looked at him and simply said 'Yes', wondering how he knew my name.

'Mark Barwell,' he declared. 'We went to school together!'

I was stunned. 'I thought I recognised you when I came in!' I said.

Then the man behind the counter introduced himself—he was Mark's brother, Nick, who was at the same school. Then Mark really blew my mind. 'How bizarre! We were only talking about you yesterday, about how we used to go to the same gym and what a laugh we used to have!'

I hadn't seen these guys for nearly 20 years! And here they were when I needed a favour and after they had been talking about me less than 24 hours before.

We caught up briefly and they gave me a discount on the van and said, 'Pop it back whenever you are finished and just put the keys through the door.' What a wonderful moment. Not to mention that the van saved me hours and hours of driving and rescued my weekend from boredom.

Entangled Down the River

I also had a fantastic experience of entangled minds while writing this book. One night I had two friends over for dinner and afterwards we got into an engaging conversation that ranged over a number of personal topics. One of the subjects we were talking about brought up memories for me of an old girlfriend, Lissa, whom I had dated eight years previously. I started fondly reminiscing about our first few dates. On our second date I had borrowed a friend's boat and we had a romantic trip down the River Thames, champagne, strawberries and sunshine—good times.

I was fully immersed in these recollections and was really enjoying reliving the experience of that time, emotions and all. Lissa and I had a wonderful two-year relationship which ended very amicably. She had moved out of the area soon after we parted ways, and I had not heard from or seen her in more than six years.

I finished recalling the stories by saying, 'I wonder what she is doing now?' I jokingly added, 'Maybe I should look on the internet to see if I can find her?' One of my pals suggested I look on the social networking site Facebook. I had never been on that particular website, although I had heard about it. I signed on, and registered to use the site at 11:01 pm, and I immediately put Lissa's name in the search box. The search returned about 25 people with the same name. Some of the people had posted photographs and some had not, and I didn't immediately see her among those with the photos. As I scrolled down the list, however, I saw one profile that could have been her, but I couldn't be sure from the photograph, for the image wasn't very clear; it was of a woman in silhouette and shadow.

My friends encouraged me to send an email anyway, so I did. As I was writing the email, I noticed that this woman's profile showed the date and time she had first joined the site and posted her profile—it was at 10:26 that night, just a half an hour before I had registered. 'Wow,' I said. 'If this is her, that's pretty wild!' I sent the email, which briefly explained my gathering with my friends and my recollections of the fun times we had had together, and sent it. During the rest of my time with my friends that night, I checked the computer for a response, but none came. The next morning, as I was conducting my routine email correspondence, a reply came. It was from Lissa. I reproduce it here verbatim:

> *Oh my god this has completely freaked me out, I have never been on facebook before and I registered last night to try and find a musician I had met. I had a look but could not find them and so logged off and went to bed. I had a dream about you last night and woke up this morning and got your e mail, oh my god.*

Needless to say, if that is not an example of entangled minds, I don't know what is. Lissa and I exchanged a few friendly emails and had a catch-up over what we had been doing over the last six years. It was a great experience.

I retold this story in one of my workshops and one of the group members, Stephanie, offered to tell her own amazing entanglement tale. She was kind enough to give me permission to share it in this book. She wrote up the account herself and it has been edited only for clarity in a few places and for length.

Stephanie's Amazing Entanglement Story

In the year 2000, I was newly married and looking for an apartment in Kingston-on-Thames, London, when luck turned my way. I had set out to go house hunting that day when my estate agent called me to tell me that an 'amazing' apartment had just come back on the books that morning and that I would seriously want to see it. Of course I was intrigued and agreed to meet her there. The apartment was part of a redeveloped area that has once been a manufacturing site for aircraft—the Sopwith Camel [a British World War I single-seat fighter plane], and I was excited about possibly living on this unique site.

The apartment delivered on all fronts, and the sellers were motivated, as they had already ex-patted to Asia. The sellers had given all rights to sign paperwork to their agent, and so my husband and I were able to quickly purchase the apartment. We were soon the proud owners of flat 87.

Three years later, out of the absolute blue, my husband returned from work one day to tell me that his employment had been moved to Singapore. The move quickly followed, with him moving there six months before me, as I had a lot to take care of to tie up loose ends in England. And, due to a very good ex-pat package, I was in a position where I didn't have to work, and so I fulfilled a long-standing dream of retraining professionally as a personal trainer and fitness coach.

Once in Singapore, I started working at a new gym, part of a British-owned chain that opened there. It had its fair share of ex-pat clientele, and thus management was very keen to employ UK-trained trainers. My training roster filled quickly, and soon I was working four to five days a week, training several British ladies among other clientele.

In order to get to know my clients better, I would chit-chat with them. Conversation would quickly turn to where I was from, where they were from, and how long they had lived in Asia. During one of these 'getting-to-know-you-better' conversations, I learned that one of my ladies had also lived in London before moving to Malaysia and then on to Singapore. We were absolutely tickled pink when we figured out that we had both lived in Kingston. A while into the conversation, she asked me where in Kingston I lived and I immediately began to describe the flat at the famous Kingston landmark where I had had the luck to live. 'No way!' she practically screamed, and then told me she had once lived in the same building. She marvelled at the odds of that, what with there being 10 million Londoners and nearly 7000 miles between Kingston and Singapore.

I was a little spooked. I was about to ask her which part of the development she had lived in, but before I even had the chance to form a coherent sentence, she said, 'We lived in the older section with the beautiful big windows and 11-foot ceilings. It was number 87 on the third floor. We lost quite a lot of money on the sale, because we were already in Asia, but luckily got to sell it quickly to some newlyweds.'

I can't remember whether I deliberately sat down or if my legs just gave way and there happened to be a bench under me. 'Those newlyweds were me and my husband,' I finally stammered. '87—we bought that flat from you!'

During the next hour, time just seemed to stand still. We went into unbelievable detail of how the apartment looked and felt, just to make absolutely sure that we were talking of the same four walls. Once I started to describe the neighbours, however, all colour drained from her face. 'This is really kind of freaking me out,' she exclaimed. 'My husband will never believe this... ever!'

That night I dug out the purchase contract on our apartment from all those years ago and it was indeed the same person—the same surname of the seller we had never met.

★ ★ ★

Entanglement has profound consequences for all of us, for it shows that we are not separate, but connected. We are part of a global consciousness, and we can dip in and out of the global field of consciousness to make connections with others. Actually, non-physical energetic communication is happening each and every moment whether you are aware of it or not. As Professor Gary Schwartz tells us,

> *One person's consciousness and energy can affect the physicality, biochemistry, cellular function and conscious experience of someone else either locally in close proximity or even hundreds or thousands of miles away.*[11]

Each of us has an individual mental and emotional field, which entangles with the larger, global 'consensus' or 'collective' field of every thought or idea that has ever been. You can call this global field the collective unconscious or think of it as the Akashic field or call it by some other name, but the bottom line is that science is able to detect evidence of it, even if conventional scientific explanations are lacking. Frontier scientists and their theories, however, are making some sense of this global field and are revealing to us ways in which we are all enmeshed in it and can use it. This new scientific perspective is why personal change and transformation are so important. It behoves each and every one of us to make sure that our subconscious and conscious thoughts and feelings are in alignment, so that we are not broadcasting mixed messages to the universe and to each other, but are clear and direct so that we can better and more easily manifest what we truly desire for ourselves.

Where Are Your Memories Stored?

A quick exercise for you. Hold out your index finger. Now point to where your memories are stored.

When I do this exercise in my workshops, most people point to their head/brain or body (as in muscle memory). Some of the examples of entangled minds and a global consciousness field that I have shared make this question very interesting. The most accurate understanding at the moment is that our memories are not stored in the brain or the body, but in some kind of memory field that is beyond the boundaries of the purely physical body.

The traditional, but now outdated, theory of memory is that when you have an experience via your five senses, biochemical and bioelectrical signals leave a trace in the your nervous system and make slight modifications to the neuron circuits in your brain cells, creating a pattern of neuronal connections that represents that memory (memories that go to your long-term memory, instead of your short-term memory, 'storage banks' that can be retrieved). When the same or sufficiently similar stimuli that laid down the original memory are received again, that occurrence activates your brain and nervous system and lights up this memory 'trace'—and you remember. This model suggests that all your memories are held in some physical location in your brain and passed onto your body by the nervous system like some sort of old-fashioned telephone exchange, where the nerve fibres are the wires and the brain is the exchange where the appropriate connections are made. Many researchers have conducted experiments to amass evidence in support of this theory. There is something to the model, as there do appear to be areas of the brain that store certain specific memories. Certain diseases or injuries can wipe out access to memories, so there does appear to be a matter-based connection via the brain. The key here is that access is different from the memories themselves. We don't know if losing access to the memory deletes the memory as well. It could be that the memory is still stored in the brain, or perhaps in a field beyond the brain. I say this because experiments show that memory may in fact be a lot more complex than first thought—it may also be a global field phenomenon.

One of the most often cited experiments that belie the 'memory stored in the brain' model was conducted by psychologist Dr Karl Lashley, who spent more than 30 years trying to trace the conditioned pathways of the brain to identify the sites of memory storage. Lashley used rats in his study that had been trained to perform specific tasks. He then began systematically removing portions of their brains in an effort to find out when they would lose the memory of those learned tasks and what part of the brain was attached to those memories. In fact, in studies with both rats and monkeys, Lashley found that he could remove almost the entire brain and still an animal did not lose its ability to remember and perform the tasks. Analogous experiments have shown that even in invertebrates, such as the octopus, specific memory traces cannot be localised. Observations on the survival of learned habits after destruction of various parts of the brain have led to the seemingly paradoxical conclusion that 'memory is both everywhere and nowhere in particular'.[12]

The fact is that there is no direct evidence that memory is stored only in the brain. Thinking that the brain is the home of our memories is the equivalent to thinking that the television set is the home of the sounds and pictures that it plays. A more up-to-date scientific understanding is that memory may also be imprinted in some kind of non-body-based information field. We now know that memory is stored in many ways, for instance as patterns of information in the body's light field and other kinds of fields, such as the zero-point field or the Akashic field, that hold the memories of everyone and everything and to which we may all have access. Your brain may not be a memory storage device as much as a tuning device, which like an antenna tunes into the wavelength or frequency of a 'memory signal' and directs it into your brain for your use.

The field model of memory has supporting evidence beyond purely biophysical experiments. It appears that when you and other people make new memories—say, when a host of people across the world all learn a new skill or come to a new understanding—then other people can learn that new skill at a quicker rate. There appears to be some kind of universal memory field, which is an aspect of the global consciousness. Evidence for this global field dates back to experiments carried out in the 1920s. You may know of the Russian scientist Ivan Pavlov because of the famous 'Pavlov's dog' experiment. But he conducted many other kinds of interesting experiments, including one in which mice were trained to run to a feeding place when an electric bell was rung. The first generation of mice required an average of 300 trials to learn this skill, but their offspring required only 100 runs to learn it, and their offspring required only 30 trials. The fourth generation learned in only 10 trials.[13] Somehow each generation of mice inherited information about the skill and so learned more quickly than the generation before it. This inheritance was not based in genetics. Genetics can influence many things, but not learned skills like how to run a particular maze to get food.

Following in Pavlov's footsteps was Australian researcher W.E. Agar and his colleagues, who tested 50 successive generations of mice over a 20-year period for skill in learning to run and exit a particular maze. The first generation was taught to run a specific maze, and then subsequent generations were introduced to the maze. They found a successive increase in the ease of learning in each subsequent generation. Even more interesting was that Agar's group also used a control group, where the mice were from a different line in which none had been taught to run this particular maze. Even this line of rats was able to learn more quickly, which suggests some kind of 'spillover' effect of the learning.[14]

How can this global learning by association be explained? One way is via global fields of information. For example, British biologist Rupert Sheldrake proposes a theory he calls morphogenesis, which includes morphic fields of information.[15] A morphic field is a sort of energetic and informational template that organises, shapes and brings coherence to all things, such that each entity in nature—ants, whales, flowers, rivers, humans—has its particular characteristics because of the information field that shapes it, much like the iron filings are shaped by the magnetic field. In this model, once a pattern or field has been established, then the species that can relate to the field can tune into it by a process called morphic resonance. As new patterns of behaviour and creativity are expressed and imprinted in that morphic field, everything that can relate to that field has access to that information and can use it. In this way, future generations can more easily learn because their ancestors have already laid down the energy and information pattern.

So your memories and thoughts are not only in your head but imprinted in a global or universal field of information, which your brain tunes in to depending on your own 'personal energy signature'. The next logical question is, what impact can you have on these information fields? Well, you are influencing them every second of every day. As you have already learned, your personal energy and information in the form of your beliefs, thoughts and emotions are broadcast outside of your body into these larger energy fields 24 hours a day.

The Effect of Intention and Thoughts on the World around Us

Your thoughts not only connect you to others, they can also impact, influence and change the world of matter. Thoughts are not material things as such but they do have bioelectrical and biochemical frequencies which have been shown to have actual effects on the material world. Let's examine some of the evidence for this.

In 1974, German physicist Fritz-Albert Popp proved that all biological systems transmit light and information via electromagnetic waves in the optical range of the spectrum. Light means photons, which are the subatomic particles of light, so Popp called these light signals 'biophotons'. They are subatomic light particles emanating from every living system, including from the cells and DNA of our bodies. Biophotons appear to be involved and even pattern the regulatory processes in our body. In some stunning research, Popp was able to correlate light emission from our bodies to disease states: cancer patients, sufferers of multiple sclerosis and people with other conditions showed lower amounts of biophoton emissions than healthy individuals.[16] It has been shown also that just one single biophoton can hold as much information as all the libraries in the world![17]

Others took up the study of biophotons, with some research aimed at seeing if our thoughts affect biophoton emissions from our bodies. Let me tell you about a couple of those studies. I'll start with a study by Slovenian researchers who wanted to know whether it was possible to show and quantifiably measure the biophotons radiating from a person's body when he or she was sending loving intentions to someone else, and if that emission rate would differ from the emission rate when that person was not sending loving intentions.[18] In their experiment, they paired people, one of which was going to send loving intentions to the other. The researchers measured the biophoton emissions from the heart of the person who was sending loving intentions to the other person—the receiver—who was in another room and sitting quietly, not doing anything in particular. This receiver was hooked up to equipment to monitor his or her heart rate via the pulse. The experiment was set up so that the sender could signal when he or she was beginning to send 'loving energy' to the receiver.

The experiment yielded some spectacular data:

❏ Baseline pre-meditation biophoton emissions from the heart of the 'sending person' were measured at 20 photons per second.
❏ When this person entered the heart-centred state, the person's biophoton emissions shot up to 37,000–45,000 photons per second.
❏ When the person was fully and deeply engaged in the loving state, his or her heart biophoton emission rate increased dramatically again, to 1,000,000 photons per second!
❏ The 'love energy and information' was registered by the receiver's heart within one to two seconds of it being sent and the receiver's pulse rate went up by 10 to 15 beats per minute!

Results such as these are not anomalous. The field of energy that carries our thoughts and emotions can actually be seen. Figure 8.2

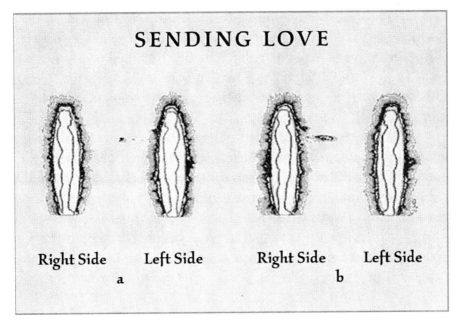

SENDING LOVE

Right Side   Left Side   Right Side   Left Side

a   b

Figure 8.2 *When one person in a coherent heart state sends loving thoughts and energy to another person, the exchange of energy can actually be imaged. Right side 'b' sending to left side and left side 'a' receiving the loving energy measured as biophoton emissions. This image is reproduced with the kind permission of Dr Konstantin Korotkov (www.korotkov.org) and. P. Krishna Madappa (www.ISSSTAOS.org, www.gdvusa.org, www.sacredoilsofkrishna.com.)*

shows visually the results of the experiment using a biophoton capture device called EPC (Electro Photon Capture). In this experiment, what was captured was the image of a person (on the right in the image, labelled 'b') in the process of intentionally sending loving thoughts to the other person (on the left, labelled 'a'). A flare of energy can be seen leaving the 'sender's' body from the heart area and being accepted by the heart of the receiver. What is even more impressive is that the sender and receiver were in two separate buildings when the experiment was conducted and the images taken! This study confirms quite clearly that when our thoughts, feelings and intentions are coherent, we create a powerful resonance energy that can affect us personally and can also influence others. This is a fine example of how the new scientific paradigm shows us the power we have to heal ourselves and the environment with our thoughts, feelings and intentions.

There are many impressive and empowering examples of how the power of intention affects matter, and below I share one from the work of William Tiller, a highly esteemed researcher who was Professor of Material Sciences at Stanford University. He and his colleagues designed four intention experiments that he characterised as the 'four experiments that will change the world'.[19] One of these experiments consisted of having four experienced meditators send an intention into a basic electronic box, which they called an Intention Imprinted Electrical Device (IIED). They wanted to see if they could 'imprint' information using human consciousness and intention into a basic electrical circuit (just like you would imprint information into a computer circuit by tapping the keyboard). Their intention was to change the pH (the acid–alkaline balance) of a water solution by one pH point with just intention and no chemical or mechanical means. Some intentions were to increase and some to decrease by 1 pH point. The four subjects would move into a deep meditative state and from there direct their intention into the box for 15 minutes. The box was then shipped 2000 miles to the other side of the country and put next to the solution and monitored. A control box with no intention was also sent.

Within a three-week period the results showed that indeed the pH of the water that had the intention-imprinted box next to it had changed by at least 1 pH point. This did not happen in the control. In case you are thinking 'One point difference, no big deal', let me remind you that changing the pH of your blood by one or two points either higher or lower and you are dead! Small changes can have significant effects. This experiment was replicated and verified by other researchers in eight different US and two European laboratories. In each experiment, the water solution changed pH by the intended amount—and the intention directed at the solution by the meditators was the only viable cause that explained this effect.

As Professor Tiller explains:

> *From this research, I and my colleagues have discovered that it is possible to make a significant change in the properties of a material substance by consciously holding a clear intention to do so. For example, we have repeatedly been able to change the*

acid/alkaline balance (pH) in a vessel of water either up or down, without adding chemicals to the water, by creating an intention to do so. This is very exciting—but even more exciting is the fact that we have been able to use a simple electronic device and actually 'store' a specific intention within its electric circuit.[20]

Professor Tiller's other experiments show that we can influence all kinds of other systems. For instance, some of his intention experiments included changing the temperature of air and water, increasing the activity of human liver enzymes, and speeding up the development of fruit flies by up to 15%.[21]

Our minds, our consciousness and our intentions are more powerful than most of us realise. What we think is possible, of course, comes right back to what we believe.

I believe we are just scraping the surface of the power of our minds, and once we awaken to that innate power, we will have a profound new understanding of ourselves which will influence everything we do. Together, as a global consciousness, our minds are having an effect on the state of the world. So, the ramification of this kind of experiment is of no small consequence, especially since some experiments show that the effect of our intentions can be cumulative.

Our consciousness appears to be entangled with the universe at all levels, from global to individual. Let's look at how mind affects DNA, the basic building block of all life.

We've all been taught that DNA is the control centre for our bodies, and conventional medicine is pinning much of its hope for curing disease on manipulating DNA. But we can already manipulate it—with our minds! Studies have shown that some individuals who have great internal coherence, such as people who practise regular meditation, are able to change the structure of DNA.

In one study a DNA sample was placed in a vial of solution that was located two to four feet in front of the meditators, who then used focused intent to influence the conformation (shape) of the DNA double helix. They were able to either unwind or rewind the helix strands using only their minds.[22] Stop and think about this for one moment. It is truly amazing. We are able with our minds to change the very building blocks of life. Our creative abilities are more or less limitless. Perhaps this result confirms what the ancient healers say: that we all have tremendous untapped self-healing capabilities and supernatural powers. The challenge for us moderns is to believe that we do, and then learn to focus our intention to use these latent capabilities. Such 'local' experiments also support other 'non-local' experiments, such as those where healers attempt to send healing energy to a person who may be thousands of miles away. Distance does not appear to matter in the efficacy of focused intention, and the non-local, global field of information provides an explanation for why it doesn't. Let's turn back now to examining the global field of consciousness. There are some experiments I want to share that may astound you.

The Gold Standard of Global Consciousness Studies

If you flipped a coin 20 times, how many heads and how many tails would you expect to get, on average? Fifty of each, right? In many areas of research, statistics rule, and so odds, or odds against chance to be more specific, play a huge role in this research. When research results consistently fall outside the bounds of chance results, researchers sit up and take notice because something important is happening—something that may defy known science. Since extraordinary claims—such as the claim that mind can affect matter—require extraordinary evidence, researchers have to be extra careful in how they design their experiments. They have to try to control for all manner of influences that could be skewing the results. And that's why some of the most intriguing and persuasive results to come out of 'psi' research all use random event generators (REGs). Let me explain.

Random event generators (REGs, which are also sometimes called random number generators) are devices that are essentially electronic coin flippers. They are devices that are designed to produce output that is purely random. Some forms of REGs produce strings of two numbers—ones and zeros—in completely random sequences. That is, they are always producing 'chance' results.

Thus, the average string of ones and zeros (and there could be millions of them in one string), over time, would produce 50% ones and 50% zeros, although in no particular pattern. If the result of a random/chance string were graphed, it would appear as a straight line. Any difference from the average (chance) would appear as a rising line if the odds against chance were in the positive range (positive numbers, in other words more than expected by chance) or as a falling line if the odds against chance were in the negative range (negative numbers, in other words less than would be expected by chance). Again, the machines are purposely designed to produce random output. If they deviated, they would have to be sent in for repair—unless there was a reason for the deviation. All of this is why REGs make such good—and objective—sense for use in psi and consciousness experiments. What better machine to use in such mind–matter experiments than an REG, which is accepted by the scientific community and designed to be purely random? If the machine is known to be calibrated and working properly and it deviates from chance during a consciousness experiment, for example, then it is almost guaranteed that the reason for the deviation is the effect of consciousness on that machine. That is why experiments using REGs have become the gold standard in much of psi and consciousness research.

There have been hundreds of experiments using REGs that clearly show that intention can affect the machine. Dean Radin, of the Noetic Sciences Institute, has both been involved in many of the most tightly controlled REG studies and also collated and reported on those done by others. Using focused intention, regular people like you and me, with no special 'psychic' abilities, have been able to influence REGs to output non-random results. Intend more ones, and more ones show up. Intend more zeros, and there are more zeros. It is not supposed to happen, but it does. In fact, Radin did a meta-analysis of more than 490 studies of this type— where people were asked to intend to change the output of REGs and were successful—and the collective odds of this result happening by chance was 50,000 to 1.[23]

Armed with this kind of result, Radin and other researchers initiated what they call the Global Consciousness Project to test whether the same effect holds for global, rather than individual, conscious influence. They set up a series of 65 REGs around the world that run 24 hours a day, with the output from each sent periodically to a computer server at Princeton University in the US, where it is analysed. Normally, they all produce purely random output. But sometimes they don't—and when they don't, it's not just one or two machines that move away from randomness to display coherence, it's all of them, at the same time. It appears that global focused consciousness 'orders' the world, or brings greater coherence to the universal field, such that this coherence shows us in the output of the REGs. Our collective mind alters both living and non-living systems.

These periods of coherence have all been correlated to world events of an emotional nature. Some of the most intense periods during which the REGs showed the effect of global consciousness by moving away from randomness and towards greater coherence include when the verdict was rendered in the O.J. Simpson trial, on the death of Princess Diana, and the terrorist attack on the United States on September 11, 2001.[24] With the advent of global media, we all learn about such events within moments of their happening. We can all share in them. We come together at the level of our consciousness, even though we are separated by oceans and mountains.

Over and over it has been shown that events that capture the world's attention and evoke strong emotions create a huge field of coherent global consciousness and that collective field reorders the world at some deep energetic level. Radin explains the process of increased global field coherence by using a simple but instructive metaphor:

> *Imagine a vast windswept ocean with scores of buoys dancing in the waves. Each buoy has a bell attached to it to alert passing ships about hidden reefs and shallows. The sounds of each buoys bell are broadcast by a radio to a land-based central receiving station. This station receives the transmissions and consolidates them to form a single collective tone reflecting the oceans grand dance. Most of the time the sound is unpatterned, similar to the*

*random tinkling one might hear from a set of wind chimes dan-
gling in the breeze. But every so often these buoys, isolated from
another by thousand of miles, mysteriously synchronise and
swell into a great harmonic chord. When this occurs, we know
that something big has affected the entire ocean.*[25]

Let me review some of the results in a bit more detail. From
August 1998 to April 2005, 185 REG events had been analysed,
with significant results showing synchronisation of human mental coherence with odds against chance of 36,400 to 1. During
the O.J. Simpson trial, there were two significant changes in
REG readouts, the first when the TV preshows started at 9am
PST on the day of the verdict and then when the verdict was
announced at 10am PST.[26] At both of those moments, the REGs
began to move away from random output towards coherent output. The odds of these changes occurring by chance were 1000
to 1. The funeral of Princess Diana created a huge spike in the
data as almost two billion people watched on TV or in person,
most sharing the same grief and shock at her passing. When the
Nobel Peace Prize-winner and Israeli prime minister Yitzhak
Rabin was murdered on November 4, 1995, the REG researchers
saw a spike in the data developing before the event and a peak in
its deviation from random at the time of his murder, suggesting
that that some kind of collective but unconscious intuitive
'knowing' was happening. This kind of precognitive field effect
was most noticeable on September 11, 2001. On the morning of
the terrorist airplane attacks in the US, there were unmistakable
changes in the REG outputs starting almost five hours before the
first plane hit the tower of the World Trade Center. Again, this
suggests an unconscious worldwide intuition about the impend-
ing event. The REGs displayed non-random behaviour for 50
hours, as events in the US were reported by news media around
the world and the people of the world watched transfixed. (See
Figure 8.3.)

Dr. Roger Nelson, director of the Global Consciousness
Project, says about these REG experiments,

*The implications of this data are huge. It means that our con-
sciousness and intentions are not confined to the skull. They are
not in the head. It's out in the world... There may be an infinite
expanse of consciousness.*

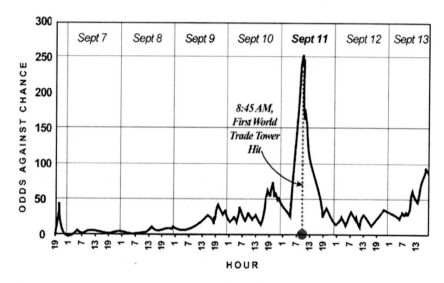

Figure 8.3   *This graph shows how for days the REGs were producing random
output, and then on the morning of September 11, 2001, they began a radical
shift towards non-randomness, correlating with the terrorist attack in the US.
Reprinted with kind permission from Dr Roger Nelson, www.noosphere.
princeton.edu/*

Can You Reduce Crime with Your Mind?

One of the most powerful examples of how our consciousness is
broadcast outside of our body is the effects shown from large-
scale meditation studies. In the 1960s Maharishi Yogi predicted
that a small amount of people experiencing a coherent meditative
state would create a significant measurable influence on coherence and orderliness throughout the surrounding society. This
became known as the Maharishi Effect and studies have shown
that if the amount of people practising transcendental meditation
is larger than 1% of the square root of the population in which it

is based, it will have a significant effect on the coherence of that society.

In the first of many studies published in peer-reviewed journals 24 cities in the US that had the transcendental meditation technique being practised by more than 1% of the square root of its population had a drop in total crime by 16% as compared to control cities.[27]

Washington, DC, has one of the highest murder rates of any city in the world. In 1991 there were over 14,000 violent crimes, averaging about 40 per day. A meditation study was carried out there between 1981 and 1986 when between 350 to 500 experienced meditators meditated twice a day. During the five-year study when the 'coherence-creating' groups were meditating in the city, the violent crime rates were reduced by almost 50%! (See Figure 8.4.) The data showed that other factors such as weather, police coverage and population changes did not account for the changes.

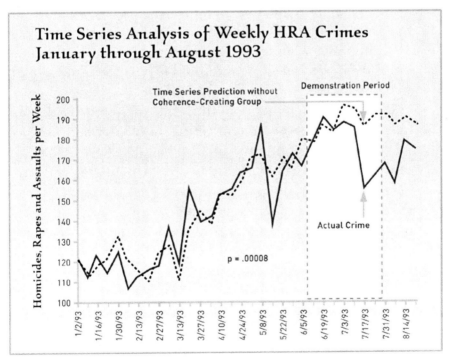

Figure 8.4 *Effects of group practice of the transcendental meditation pro-gramme on preventing violent crime in Washington, DC: Results of the National Demonstration Project, June–July, 1993. Social Indicators Research 1999 47:153-201. Image reproduced with kind permission of the Maharishi University. www.mum.edu*

So it is clear that the field effect created by the consciousness of the meditators dramatically affected the 'mindset field' and therefore the behaviours of the would-be criminals.

Make Intentions Part of Your Life

Start now to use the power of your mind and intentions. Each and every day intend for your day to go well, for you to be in flow, to see opportunities, to have fun and to be full of vitality. Before you eat, intend for your food to create masses of physical, mental and emotional energy. Make intention as natural a part of your life as breathing is. Before any meeting, event, family visit, any conversation, intend for it to go well and for you to enjoy it, learn from it, be in harmony with the situation, be in flow and relaxed about the outcomes of situations. Remember, get in a heart-based emotional state like gratitude, love or appreciation or just feeling really good and happy to amplify the energy of your intentions. Your intentions are powerful and easy to integrate into your life. Use them and monitor your results.

The examples throughout this chapter show us that the power of our mind–body system is truly amazing when we know how to access it, program it and use it. They also show us that even when we don't know how to consciously focus and use intention to affect matter, we are doing so anyway—unconsciously via the field of global consciousness. Whether the influence we seek is local or global, the fact remains that when we increase our coherence to fully realise and use the power of our minds, we can change ourselves and the world around us.

That collective 'we' includes you! Each and every day of your life, you are broadcasting your beliefs, thoughts and feelings, your 'personal energy signature', through the invisible energy and information fields into your body, your local environment, the world and the universe. As you have already learned, no matter how many affirmations or positive thoughts you project through your conscious mind, the real energy vibration you are broadcasting comes from your subconscious. It trumps your conscious mind because it is the repository of your deepest beliefs. You can't fool your subconscious. That's why the change technique I will be teaching you is so important. You can change your thoughts (as in using positive affirmations or making a New Year resolution) but until you truly transform your beliefs, change is unlikely to stick.

The energy and information that flow from your mind–body system shape every aspect of your life. In 1999 I had the pleasure to meet former NASA astronaut Edgar Mitchell, the sixth man to walk on the moon. Dr Mitchell explained:

> *We create our own reality because our inner subconscious reality draws us into situations from which we learn. We experience it as strange things happening to us and we meet the people in our lives we need to learn from. And so we create these circumstances at a very deep metaphysical and subconscious level.*

Increasing coherence between your subconscious and conscious minds—bringing them into alignment—is crucial to creating the life you say you want. When your 'two minds' are in alignment, change can happen quickly and almost effortlessly—some might even say magically.

But for most of us, change is difficult and tiresome. Or at least we believe it is. So before we 'hit the change button' and since knowledge is power, let's take a look in the next chapter at how we change, develop and evolve. And let's also explore the massive difference between vertical and horizontal personal development.

Key Points

- ❏ An individual human mind is part of a collective global mind.
- ❏ Every human being is interconnected and entangled with every other human being via the global consciousness field.
- ❏ Your intentions can manifest into a physical reality.
- ❏ At a mostly unconscious metaphysical level, we create our own reality.

9

CHANGE IS THE SMART OPTION

It is not the strongest of the species that survives, nor the most intelligent, but the one most responsive to change.

Charles Darwin

Today our world is changing at an extraordinary rate. Consider that just 100 years ago we did not have television or computers and less than 10% of the homes in the west had a telephone. Today we have over one billion internet users and the amount of information at our fingertips dramatically exceeds what has been available to every other generation in our entire human history.

From the invention of the wheel (approx 3500 BC) to the 1980s, the world was doubling its knowledge approximately every five years. By the year 2000 the world was doubling its knowledge every nine to ten months, and in 2010 that figure had moved to every six to seven months. You may remember back in Chapter 6 where we discussed the power of super computers. Let's go over that again and add a very important extra piece.

Imagine all 7 billion human beings on planet Earth with a hand-held calculator performing a calculation every five seconds for sixty hours. The world's most powerful computers, called super computers, can perform the same amount of 7 billion calculations every five seconds for sixty hours in just one second. We are at the age of quantum computing. Now imagine a super computer running for a trillion years. That in itself is a mind blower, but wait, there's more: a quantum computer could perform the same amount of calculations as a super computer running for a trillion years in just one hour! Now, I don't know about you, but I cannot even get close to getting my head around that one.

What that means, though, is when the quantum computing technology is fully developed, the world will be doubling its knowledge almost every day and the suggestion is that this technology will be with us within the next three to five years.[1]

Interestingly, research into scientific and technological developments that were conducted at Stanford University also suggests a similar rate of expansion. A computer program plotted the speed of advances in technological developments starting at approximately 5000 BC and continuing until today. The prediction plot line took a steep upturn from 1975 onwards, and in 2012 it goes completely off the chart. Hang onto your hats, folks.

We simply have to change our belief systems in order to keep up with the pace of change and to allow us to fully express who and what we are. As a Chinese proverb says, 'We will end up where we are going if we do not change direction.'

Personal Change and Development

We all have aspects of ourselves that we want to change: habits and predispositions that we know aren't serving us, and unrealised talents we keep promising ourselves we will explore and develop. Life is about change, and yet many of us realise that life is passing us by while we're following the old adage, 'The more things change, the more they stay the same.' It takes more than willpower and positive thinking to change—and even to discover what it is about ourselves that we want to change. It takes insight into what we might call the 'hidden' aspects of ourselves. Our minds might tell us one thing, but our hearts are whispering something else. To whom do we most often listen? Why? And if we truly do desire change, how can we best achieve it so that it is long-lasting and life-affirming?

One way is to consult an expert, such as a coach or a psychologist. They tend to use psychological assessments to help us gain insight and increase our awareness of our personality strengths and weaknesses, and personal styles and tendencies. These assessments aim to give us more understanding of our behavioural patterns and to help us foster greater behavioural flexibility, increasing our opportunities for growth. However, it is possible for you to know yourself more deeply than you already do without using 'canned' personality tests or consulting an expert. You are your own best expert. Let's explore some proven strategies about how best to delve into the core of you—via your conscious and unconscious minds—and tease out the secrets of yourself. It will help if you understand the more or less universal human development stages, so you can assess where you are and how you are doing. The information in this chapter prepares you for the next chapter, where I teach you the Mind–Body Belief-Change Technique.

Exploring the Stages of Human Development

Starting in the 1960s, psychologists began to focus on how adults develop, advancing from a baby's self-centred view of the world to an adult understanding and realisation that we are far more expansive than our 'personality self'. Human development was mapped out into what became known as stages, world views or meaning-making systems. I will use the term 'stages'. As we move through each stage of development, we acquire more comprehensive and effective strategies for dealing with complexity, as that stage means we have 'evolved' in deeper and more expansive ways of engaging ourselves and the world. The earlier stages of development are often grouped into what's called the 'first tier', and the later or higher stages are referred to as the 'second tier'. The highly respected developmental expert and former Professor of Psychology Clare Graves said that when a person moves to the second tier, they 'go through a momentous leap of meaning'.[2]

Human development is mapped in lateral and vertical directions. Lateral growth occurs by learning new knowledge and skills, through education and schooling and the experiences of daily life. We develop laterally as we strengthen the different types of intelligences we all have, as identified by Harvard psychologist Howard Gardner, such as in IQ, emotional, logical-mathematical, musical, body-kinaesthetic, spatial, interpersonal, intrapersonal and other skills. Vertical development is much less common in the general population. It refers to the ability to shift our world view—to be able to see the world through new eyes, so to speak—and to change our interpretation of our experiences and perceptions as we move through life. Vertical development increases our openness and level of awareness, fosters our ability to make sense of broader and more diverse perspectives, and expands our ability to both influence our world and integrate our personal experiences.

As we ascend to the second tier and the later stages of development, and as we move from lateral to vertical development, we increase our likelihood of accessing more of our personal potential and deeper levels of understanding, effectiveness and wisdom. After all, human development is really about the state of human consciousness, which means it directly affects our ability to transform what we think and feel about ourselves.

To make the meaning of these stages and tiers clear, I'll use an extended metaphor. Imagine there is a forest that you walk through regularly to get some exercise and relax. Even though there are many different paths you could take, no matter which one you select, the scenery is pretty much the same: trees, bushes, birds, squirrels. It's a pleasant and relatively easy walk, with a few hills to negotiate, and it quickly becomes familiar and comfortable. In fact, it becomes so familiar that you begin to lose sight of its details, taking the diversity of the forest for granted and walking through it without focusing your awareness.

Now imagine that one day you feel intrigued by a new trail you just noticed, and you veer off your normal route and take it. You soon discover that it's a steeper path, leading up a small mountain, but you stay on it despite the extra effort it takes. You follow it upward for a while, until you come to the top, where you break out of the forest growth and have a panoramic view.

As you look around, you can see some of the familiar paths below in the forest and how they connect. You can see that beyond one edge of the forest there is a valley, and that a river flows through the valley. You can even make out a few towns. You have a whole new appreciation of the forest itself and of how it is situated in the larger landscape.

Early development stages, first-tier development and lateral development correlate with the familiar, with how we grow comfortable with our world, our life and our behaviours. We keep doing the same comfortable things, and we don't venture too far beyond the existing boundaries of our knowledge and emotions. We are not expanding our consciousness very much. In contrast, when you veer off the familiar path, you might find yourself on a more challenging journey, but the pay-off is a dramatically expanded view of life, wider horizons of experience, a more accurate and detailed knowledge of yourself and how you fit into the world and so on. This expansion represents the benefits and gifts of the later developmental stages, the second tier of development and vertical development.

Developmental stages provide a generalised way of understanding how people interpret events and, therefore, how they are likely to act in various situations. Each of us has a vast array of potential responses, behaviours and tendencies, and yet we tend to display the same ones over and over. It is part of what gives us an identifiable and stable personality to others, but ultimately we fall into a rut of learned behaviours and responses that may keep us from experiencing the world as fresh and exciting. Our growth stagnates. To change and evolve, most of us first have to want to change, and then we have to find effective ways to change our beliefs, for it is our beliefs that either restrict or expand our potential. Because beliefs reside in the unconscious, change means we have to align our unconscious and conscious selves. However, your consciousness is not static, and it too can grow and develop.

The Stages of Human Consciousness

Most developmental theories divide the spectrum of human consciousness into four tiers: pre-conventional, conventional, post-conventional and transpersonal. (See Figure 9.1.) Pre-conventional represents the stage of consciousness of an infant, who is largely self-absorbed and does not relate to the perspective of others. As the child begins to learn the norms and rules of the culture, he or she moves into the conventional stage. This stage of consciousness represents a feeling of inclusion, of identifying with and belonging to a group,

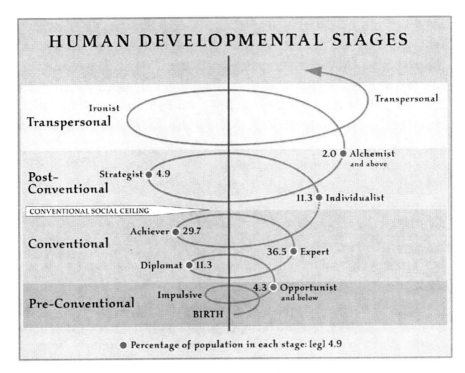

Figure 9.1   *Bill Torbet, Professor Emeritus of Management at the Carroll School of Management at Boston College and one of the most well-respected developmental theorists, modelled the stages of human consciousness and development, and estimated the percentage of the population at each stage. The stages in this model are given labels to differentiate one from another, just like 1, 2, 3 etc. The labels themselves are not important in this discussion.*

tribe or nation. That group provides a feeling of safety and security, so anyone or anything outside of that group tends to be excluded or questioned. As a person continues to develop, he or she may reach the post-conventional stage of consciousness, where his or her sense of identity widens to include people that may be unlike him- or herself. The person is open and accepting of people no matter what their race, colour, gender, nationality and so on. If a person continues along a path of growth, he or she may move into a state of transpersonal consciousness, where he or she identifies with and cares for all beings, human and non-human, and feels that there is one, integrated cosmos of which he or she is a part. It's a more 'universal' consciousness.

Each stage in this model has its own fundamental belief structures that guide the people at that level as to their style and range of thinking, feeling and acting. Generally speaking, a person who has reached the later stages of development can understand the earlier world views, but a person at an earlier stage has difficulty understanding the later stages. As Figure 9.1 shows, approximately 80% of people in modern society function at the conventional stage, and only about 10% to 20% demonstrate post-conventional world views. Very few people have reached the transpersonal stage of consciousness.

Going Up?

Vertical development first and foremost starts with assessing and updating your belief systems: your idea of who and what you are, and your reason for being. For the most part, the shift from stage to stage vertically does not happen suddenly, but is the result of continuous small steps forward in your journey of self-actualisation and personal evolution. Change is often accelerated by personal practice and by coming into contact with people who are already at the stage you are seeking to achieve or are already moving towards it. They can help 'show you the way', so to speak.

With our understanding today of the significance of the mind–body relationship and of how 'energy psychology' (defined in the next chapter) can facilitate the processes of change, you can make more rapid progress in your vertical development. This is a time in human history when such progress is being asked of us, not only for our personal benefit but also so that we can meet the challenges of our world and change it for the better. The tools are available on a wide scale to help us achieve the highest positive expression of ourselves and of our culture, nation and even the world. As Drs Ervin Laszlo and Jude Currivan explain in their book *Cosmos*:

> *We are… living in a momentous era when powerful evolutionary and indeed revolutionary processes are playing out. We are individually and collectively waking up as if from a long slum-*

*ber of amnesia. Not only are we acknowledging our innate abil-
ities to perceive on non-local levels, but our awareness is
expanding beyond the limitations of our personality-based sense
of self.[3]*

The most efficient and effective way to achieve personal change
and development is to undertake a programme of what is called an
'integral practice' that is based on four key areas:

- ❏ Exercise and nutrition
- ❏ Meditation
- ❏ Cognitive development
- ❏ Psychodynamic practices (clearing and updating your
  subconscious)

Exercise

Obviously, it makes good sense to honour your physical body
through grooming, eating nutritiously, supplementing your diet
with good-quality vitamins and minerals, being fully hydrated and
getting enough exercise.

If you had only one option for choosing a physical fitness
activity, I would recommend resistance training, and the best form
of resistance training is weight training. Why is this so good?
Because weight training is the best way to deal with, and even to
reverse, the effects of biological ageing. Studies have shown that
after six months of weight training just three times per week for
twenty minutes each session, the indicators of biological ageing
were reduced by twelve years![4]

When most people think of weight training, they think of the
stereotypical image of bodybuilders straining to build huge muscles. Forget that. The truth is that the health benefits of weight
training go way beyond any other form of exercise. Here is a short
list of some of the benefits of weight training (and of certain types
of resistance training):

❏ Strengthens your muscles, tendons and ligaments, helping you achieve a strong, balanced posture and an increase in strength and endurance for everyday tasks.

❏ Raises your basal metabolic rate by as much as 15%, which causes you to burn more calories throughout the day, well after your exercise is done and even while you're sleeping. Weight training can make your body burn up to 300 additional calories a day (for someone who normally burns 2000 calories per day), so over time, it can lead to significant fat loss.

❏ Strengthens your bones, reducing your risk of developing osteoporosis.

❏ Decreases your resting blood pressure.

❏ Improves your balance and coordination.

❏ Increases your blood level of HDL cholesterol (the good type).

❏ Enhances immune system functioning.

In fact, weight or resistance training has been proven to have a positive affect on insulin resistance, resting metabolism, blood pressure, body fat and gastrointestinal transit time, factors that are linked to illnesses such as diabetes, heart disease and cancer.[5] In a nutshell, weight or resistance training helps keeps you youthful.

Having had a previous career in the health and fitness industry, I know only too well that many people start an exercise programme with high enthusiasm, only to lose interest and discipline after a while. This behaviour is usually based on a belief, learned in youth, that exercise is hard work and boring. This is a belief that can be changed, as you will soon learn. In addition, many of us are overscheduled, and we think we cannot possibly undertake one more activity. However, if you examine your life, you will find that you usually make time for what is important to you. Changing your belief structure can make exercise an enjoyable part of your life. You'll be surprised how quick and easy change is.

Huge Benefits, No Side Effects

Have a look at the list of psychological and physiological benefits below. If I were to show you how to achieve those benefits without any side effects or cost to you, would you do it?

Psychological benefits:

- ❏ Increases serotonin level, influencing mood and behaviour
- ❏ Increases alpha brain waves leading to increased left- and right-hemisphere integration and whole-brain functioning
- ❏ Increases activity in the left frontal lobe, increasing happiness and calmness
- ❏ Improves focus and concentration
- ❏ Improves learning and memory
- ❏ Develops intuition
- ❏ Decreases restless thinking
- ❏ Enhances inner peace, happiness and contentment
- ❏ Increases perceptual ability and motor performance
- ❏ Enhances the harmony of body, mind and spirit

Physiological benefits:

- ❏ Increases blood flow and slows heart rate
- ❏ Creates a deeper level of relaxation
- ❏ Reduces blood pressure
- ❏ Reduces the activity of viruses
- ❏ Lowers cholesterol levels
- ❏ Reduces the risk of cardiovascular disease
- ❏ Decreases the ageing process
- ❏ Decreases stress-related cortisol
- ❏ Strengthens the immune system
- ❏ Helps a variety of medical conditions: asthma, type 2 diabetes, PMS and chronic pain
- ❏ Increases blood flow to the brain, creating higher brain function
- ❏ Relaxes the nervous system

If you answered yes, then welcome to meditation. Contrary to what some people believe, meditation is not a religious practice. It is a health-related relaxation and stress-reducing practice. There are so many benefits to meditation that if a drug offered the same results and doctors did not prescribe it for their patients, they would be struck off the medical register. The list goes on and on, making it obvious why meditation is an integral part of a self-development programme.

Cognitive Development

Cognitive development is the use of our reason and logic—the use of our thinking mind—and it constitutes the third part of an integral practice. We have to have a cognitive understanding of our choices to have the motivation to act on a decision, feel what it means, identify what we gain from it, determine why we need that benefit and care that we attain it. You gain greater cognitive ability through self-education and honing a better understanding of who you are and of the world you live in. The ways to increase your cognitive abilities are extremely varied, so I will highlight only a few.

Beyond schooling, taking courses and other traditional knowledge-acquisition and skill-enhancing routes, ways to improve your thinking and decision-making skills include:

❑ Learning through observation of your own acts and their consequences and those of others (basically, learning through experience).

❑ Exposing yourself to rich environments, with lots of novel input that 'broadens your horizons' and allows you to consider new ways of acting, thinking and doing; novelty not only stimulates imagination but may sharpen cognitive abilities throughout your life.

❑ Exercise your brain by doing crosswords or other kind of puzzles, and by learning a new skill, such taking up a musical instrument or learning a new language; turn off the television and pick up a book or stimulating magazine.

Psychodynamic Practices

Psychodynamics refers to the workings of your psyche or mind—what's going on subconsciously that is hidden and may be hindering you. The Emotional Balance Technique© (see Chapter 7) and the Gamma Belief Change Technique I will share with you in the next chapter are psycho dynamic in nature, so I will address this approach to personal change there.

★ ★ ★

These four areas build a powerful transformative practice. It has been shown that 'cross-training' in these four integral areas is a far faster and more efficient way to grow and develop than doing only one practice on its own. For example, a research study of a Buddhist meditation practice known as Vipassana, also called insight meditation, tested three groups: one group practised Vipassana meditation only, a second group practiced Vipassana and added weight-training exercise to their weekly routine, and the third group did neither (they were the control group). The group that performed Vipassana and did weight training developed a deeper meditation practice than did the meditation-only group, as judged by a group of master Vipassana monks.[6] The point here is not about learning to meditate more deeply, although that certainly is a worthy goal, but it is about undertaking proven ways to speed up your personal development. Regular exercise, eating and hydrating well, meditation and learning combined with the Emotional Balance Technique© and the Gamma Belief-Change Technique© is a sure-fire way of being 'all that you can be'.

You are about to learn how to transform your beliefs in every area of your life using the Gamma Belief Change Technique© and Gamma Brain Technique©. Are you ready?

Key Points

❏ The pace of change is faster than at any other time in history.
❏ Human development is mapped out in stages: the higher the stage, the greater the level of consciousness.
❏ An integral practice is the most effective way to foster personal development.

10

CHANGE YOUR SUBCONSCIOUS BELIEFS

To perceive the world differently, we must be willing to change our belief systems, let the past slip away, expand our sense of now, and dissolve the fear in our minds.

Professor William James,
American psychologist and philosopher

As we have seen, the majority of our belief systems are stored at a subconscious level. You can change some beliefs consciously by upgrading your knowledge with books, courses and ongoing education and study. When you were a child, for example, you didn't have to use any subconscious change processes to update your beliefs about Father Christmas, the Easter bunny or the earth being flat. But as an adult, the belief programmes you are running about your sense of self and your view of the world are more or less fixed unless you change them at a subconscious level. So let's move finally into how you do that.[1]

Most people have been conditioned to think of change as difficult and threatening rather than as exciting, liberating and self-affirming. It's a truism that, as the old saying goes, 'The only people who like change are cashiers and wet babies.' But that is the mantra of the old scientific paradigm. Now that you know about the new scientific paradigm—that everything is made up of energy and information fields that are responsive to new energy and information inputs—you can more easily realise how your current belief programs can be easily and quickly updated.

The new paradigm emerged partly from a modern field of psychology known as 'energy psychology'. It uses the latest principles of how your mind–body system transfers information and energy, as I have laid out for you in the previous chapters. At a conference of the Association for Comprehensive Energy Psychology (ACEP2005), this new field was defined as follows:

> *Energy psychology is a family of mind–body interventions clin-*
> *ically observed to help with a range of psychological concerns,*
> *through directly and methodically treating the human vibra-*
> *tional matrix. This matrix includes the biofield that envelopes*
> *the body and the energy pathways.*[2]

You will now be working at the level of your biofield and the vibrational matrix that encodes your current belief patterns. So, before we move into the process of belief change, let us look at some of the old-paradigm patterns versus new-paradigm ones so that you will be completely confident in the change process you are about to learn. You can then deeply embrace the new belief that your subconscious patterns are about to easily change in life-empowering ways.

Old Paradigm

Beliefs take a long time to change, and the longer you have had a belief the more time it takes to revise it. This outdated view goes back to the early days of psychology and neuroscience, when scientists told us erroneously that our brains are hardwired, static and fixed like some sort of machine made purely of physical parts.

New Paradigm

Beliefs change easily because our brains are continually forming new neural connections and are extremely adaptable. Metaphorically, changing subconscious beliefs is like revising a document in a computer. It doesn't take any longer to change a document that has been in your computer for two years than it does one that has been there for five minutes. Like a computer program, your brain is configuring and storing patterns of energy and information. If you change the configuration, you change what is recorded, stored and available for activation.

Old Paradigm

Changing old behaviours, thought patterns and belief systems is emotionally difficult and even painful. This belief grows out of healing interventions stemming back to Sigmund Freud, who taught that for people to heal and grow, they had to recover hidden memories (usually painful ones they were avoiding) from their past and relive them with more awareness and insight. By doing so, we are supposed to be better able to make wiser choices if similar situations arise in our lives again. This may be true to some extent, as awareness surely is healing. However, awareness on its own does not stop the subconscious 'tape' playing. It took us a lifetime to store all the myriad beliefs about everyday life that make up our sense of self and our world view. If we followed Freud's path it might take a lifetime to access them all—which is why 'talking therapy' often takes years and is very limited in its results.

New Paradigm

We know that our belief systems at the most fundamental level are specific patterns of energy and information within the body. Working with the matrix system of the body allows us to change our beliefs quickly and effectively.

Old Paradigm

In order to change, you must bring the limitation or issue to consciousness. This old-paradigm declaration is not unlike the one Freud taught. But as you now know, your conscious mind is far less powerful an information processor than is your subconscious mind. If we could easily change because we brought an issue to conscious awareness, then we would all succeed in keeping our New Year resolutions. We'd all be thin, rich and happy—whatever. No matter how much you logically analyse how your problems stem from a tough childhood or a series of failed relationships, you can certainly gain insight but you probably won't get to the root beliefs that contribute to a pattern of self-limiting behaviours.

Conscious insight can be very healing, but in terms of lasting belief change, it's a bit like trying to change the hard drive on your computer by becoming aware of how to use your word-processing program. You are dealing with the wrong part of the system.

New Paradigm

The most efficient way to change subconscious beliefs is to have the latest understanding of your mind–body 'operating system' and to use a set of energetic psychology tools that provide a way to change deep-seated beliefs. It's also necessary to have a direct feedback mechanism that reveals if you have completely integrated the new beliefs. With the appropriate techniques, you can change your internal energy and information fields quickly and painlessly without needing to analyse and dissect your 'issues' logically through your conscious awareness.

Old Paradigm

All change comes through a mind that is only in the brain.

New Paradigm

The doorway to your subconscious mind is your body. Energy psychology tells us that our bodies encode everything we believe. As the mind goes, so goes the body. Our ego mind is a master at masking truth and keeping us from what we might not want to see. Our body is usually the truth teller. Therefore, it is through the body that we can most quickly and objectively access the realm of our subconscious. And this is where we start in the belief-change process, so let me take a moment to explain the body-oriented 'tool' called kinesiology, and specifically mind–body kinesiology. You will be using your body to change your beliefs, so the next sections are crucial to your successful application of the Gamma Belief Change Technique©.

Letting Your Body Talk for You: Mind–Body Kinesiology

The most effective way to find out whether you believe something at the root subconscious level is using a simple biofeedback muscle test from the field of kinesiology. Kinesiology is the study of how the body, and especially the muscles, move.

Science tells us that unresolved emotional conflicts, psycho-emotional trauma and limiting beliefs from early childhood and beyond remain active in our subconscious mind throughout adult life, and our limbic system (a core emotional centre of the brain that deals with motivation, behaviour etc.) communicates these conflicts and beliefs to our body via our autonomic nervous system.[3] When there is a disconnect between what you believe subconsciously and what you say or do, a stress response results, moving from the limbic system into the body. Your body responds to that stress signal. Maybe you blush. Maybe you stammer. Maybe your stomach tightens. Maybe you feel fear or anger. Maybe you do any of the other things that reveal you are under stress. The fact is that some way or another, stress results from the collision that is taking place within you, and it is registered in your body.

Kinesiology capitalises on this cascade of physical events, using it as a way to access the subconscious, through what is called 'muscle testing'. The cause of the stress may be unconscious, but the results are physical and show up as weakened muscle responses. The collision between our subconscious and conscious minds literally weakens us as electrical signals become less ordered and efficient, resulting in reduced muscle strength. Complete agreement between your subconscious and conscious minds equals a strong muscle response, whereas a deep disconnect between the two equals a weak muscle response. To test a muscle, you have only to hold a belief in mind and then test your muscle response. It's that easy. And that's why muscle testing has become the ideal tool to obtain feedback concerning the state of arousal of a person's nervous system.

Muscle testing was first bought to the west more than 40 years ago by Dr George Goodheart, the founder of Applied Kinesiology. Over the years, it has been adopted as a quick and effective diagnostic tool by medical doctors, chiropractors, osteopaths, dentists, psychologists, nutritionists, massage therapists and others. The amount of energy going to a muscle can be specifically measured using what is called a bio-kinesiometer. This device clearly shows that when a person has negative thoughts, his or her muscle output weakens. It is important for you to realise that in the belief-change process, although I use the terms 'strong response' or 'weak response', you are not testing muscle strength per se but rather the amount of electromagnetic signal or energy flowing to the muscle in relation to what is being held in the mind. Validation of this kind of muscle testing was demonstrated by Dr Daniel Monte and colleagues, with their findings reported in the *Journal of Perceptual and Motor Skills* in 1999.[4] Theirs is a technical explanation, so here I will conclude by sharing a more accessible explanation from Professor William Tiller:

> *Kinesiology is a type of biofeedback utilising muscle responses to detect stressors within the body. Kinesiology uses manual monitoring of specific muscles which may lock and hold strong or unlock and give away to determine chemical or other energetic imbalances of stressors, not only within the muscles themselves but also within interfacing subconscious body systems. These systems include not only the generally recognised autonomic and proprioceptive feedback of the nervous system, but also the subconscious emotional and mental processes underlying our feelings and thoughts.[5]*

Now that you know about kinesiology, it's time to use it to discover where your subconscious and conscious beliefs are in conflict. If you have a bit of trouble believing this method will work, you are not alone. Some years ago, I introduced an old friend of mine to muscle testing and he immediately doubted it would work. We were gym training partners and he was a very strong guy. He didn't believe his muscles would ever test weak. However, he allowed me to demonstrate, and I took him through the first three steps, which I will share with you below, and he was shocked that he could not consciously control his arm muscle when thinking of a stressful situation or speaking aloud a name that was not his. I mention this to let you know that doubt is okay. This method works and, rather ironically, your belief in it or lack thereof will not actually make a difference.

Gamma Belief Change Technique©

You need a partner to undertake the Gamma Belief Change Technique©. In the instructions below, I will call the person whose subconscious beliefs are being tested the 'receiver' and the person who is doing the muscle testing the 'partner'. The receiver should be in a calm state and well hydrated before being muscle tested.

1. Establishing communication with your subconscious using muscle testing.
2. Constructing a belief statement.
3. Testing the belief statement to see if the belief is fully integrated into your subconscious.
4. Integrating the beliefs if required.

Note: There are four main parts of the belief-change process: There are other intermediate steps depending on your responses. I will introduce you to the muscle testing and integration processes in this chapter, using belief statements I have provided, and then I will explain how to construct your own empowering belief statements at the end of the chapter. It is a good idea to read through the rest of this chapter to familiarise yourself with the exercises before actually beginning the belief-change process.

Part One: Establishing Communication with Your Subconscious Mind Using Muscle Testing

By establishing a connection with your subconscious, you are sure to be working at the deep inner level of being where your belief programs are stored and where they can be changed.

1. The receiver (hereafter in the instructions, I will simply say 'you') stands upright with your head facing forward and your chin parallel to the floor.

2. Now raise your arm up (it doesn't matter which one), directly out to your side at about shoulder height, parallel to the floor and have your partner (for convenience's sake, I will just say 'he' throughout the instructions) support your arm by placing his thumb under your wrist and his fingers on top of your wrist. He should be gently supporting you, not applying undue pressure. He also gently places his other hand on your shoulder to focus attention on the muscle you will contract. See Figure 10-1.

3. Speak your name out loud in a simple declarative sentence, such as 'My name is Stephanie.' Your partner then cues you with the word 'Hold', alerting you that he is about to muscle test. He gently but firmly pushes down on your wrist as if to move your

Figure 10.1   *The starting position for the muscle testing part of the belief-change process: head held up and facing straight ahead, one arm comfortably extended out to your side. Your partner gently supports your wrist and lightly rests his hand on your shoulder.*

arm towards the floor and you should contract your shoulder muscle to resist his push. His cue 'Hold' makes it very clear to your conscious mind that you are contracting your shoulder muscle at the right time. This is not a test to see how hard you can resist or if your partner can force your arm downwards. All your partner wants to do is sense if there is a lock of the muscle or a weakening in the muscle. It may take a few 'test runs' for you to be able to sense what weak and strong mean for you.

So again, you speak your name, your partner cues you that he is about to muscle test you, and then he applies gentle to medium downward pressure to test the energy going to that muscle. He should find that your arm is strong, with the muscle locked, because the statement of your name was 'true' and so presents no internal conflict within your mind–body system. Remember, generally speaking, a gentle to medium firm pressure is all that is needed to test your muscle; this is not a strength test. Now rest your arm.

Note: If you do not get the expected response for this or any other exercise (here, your muscle tested weak when you said your real name), you might want to jump ahead and review the 'Some Pointers about Muscle Testing' section below. Then come back and try again.

4. After a brief rest, raise your arm again and this time make a statement saying a false name, perhaps a name of the opposite sex, such as: 'My name is Fred.' Lightly contract your shoulder muscle as your partner cues you and then gently presses on your wrist to test the energy in the muscle. He will find that your muscle is weaker and does not lock, because your body feels the conflict and therefore stress of the false claim you just made about your name. (See Figure 10.2.)
5. Now follow exactly the same muscle testing process while you are thinking about a pleasurable experience. You don't speak this out loud. Just think of a positive experience you have had, reliving it as fully as you can. You should test strong for this.

Figure 10.2

6. Finally, repeat the procedure while you think of a stressful, hurtful or negative experience. You will find that a stressful experience shows itself as a weak muscle response no matter how hard you try to keep your arm strong.

Some Pointers about Muscle Testing

If you had any difficulty with the process, don't worry. It's probably because you are new to it. As with any other activity, you get better with practice. However, there can be several kinds of 'anomalous' responses with muscle testing as you first begin to set up communication with your subconscious, so let's review them.

❏ If there is no clear difference between a strong and a weak muscle response, then either your partner may need to apply slightly more pressure so that you and he can clearly feel the difference between strong and weak responses, or your partner may be overzealous and applying too much pressure. The pressure needed varies with each person on the receiving end of the test, so you and your partner may need to experiment a little to get a clear signal.

❑ Occasionally in my workshops I have seen people test weak for their own name and strong for a false name. Or they test weak or strong for both name statements. Either of these occurrences can be a sign of dehydration, or a distortion in your energy system. If this happens, simply stop and take a drink of water, tap the nine meridian points a few times each, and then retest.

Part Two: Making Empowering Belief Statements

Just as important as muscle testing properly and getting a clear response is making empowering belief statements. I will teach you to make your own statements at the end of this chapter, but generally the criteria for empowering belief statements are that they be:

❑ In the present tense.
❑ Unambiguous, meaning you are testing for a single belief and not a string of them in one statement. Sometimes closely related terms work well together, as in the second and third statements in the bulleted list below, but generally you want each statement to be about a single context.
❑ Succinct, meaning that the shorter and more direct the belief statement, the better.

Below is a list of empowering belief statements that are common ones to begin with. You will be practising the belief-change process using these, to see if you are subconsciously in alignment with these foundational beliefs.

❑ I love myself unconditionally.
❑ I deeply accept and appreciate myself.
❑ It's healthy and positive for me to be a success.
❑ I deserve to be a success.
❑ My body heals itself naturally and efficiently.
❑ I love every part of my body.
❑ I live my life full of vitality, energy and enthusiasm.
❑ Change is easy for me.

❏ I am ready for a loving, intimate and passionate relationship in my life now.

❏ I set healthy boundaries in my relationships.

❏ I am true to my feelings in my relationships.

❏ I have a good balance of logic and intuition.

❏ Every part of me is ready, willing and able to have lots of money now.

❏ I deserve to be financially wealthy.

❏ I am sensible with and in control of my finances.

❏ I receive and give money with gratitude.

There are hundreds of other belief statements you can test, and I have provided lists categorised by subject in Appendix C. For now, let's practise the belief-change process using some of the statements on this list. First let's muscle test these belief statements.

Part Three: Muscle Test the Belief Statements

1. Head forward, chin parallel to the ground, arm extended out to your side.
2. Speak the belief statement aloud: I love myself unconditionally.
3. Your partner says 'Hold', and then muscle tests the statement.
4. Your muscle will either lock or not (strong response, meaning your subconscious believes this statement, or weak response, meaning your subconscious is not in alignment with this belief).

If you test strong, then you can go to another part of the belief-change process, 'When You Test Strong', described below. If you tested weak, skip down to the 'When You Test Weak' section.

When You Test Strong

If you tested strong to the belief statement, your subconscious and conscious minds are in alignment. However, they may not be in 100% alignment. You may only weakly believe that statement. To make lasting change in your life, you want a vibrant and robust alignment. This is simply done by asking a question and muscle testing.

Checking that the Belief Is 100% Integrated

1. Assume the normal muscle testing posture. You now say: 'This belief is integrated at 100%.' He then says 'Hold' and muscle tests you.
2. If you test strong, then the belief is fully true for you and congruent with your subconscious and conscious belief system.
3. If you test weak, you are experiencing an inner conflict. The belief statement you tested for earlier is not 100% integrated. Don't be alarmed! Of the thousands of people for whom I have tested this belief statement ('I love myself unconditionally'), not many were in alignment with it subconsciously. 'Unconditionally' is a powerful word.
4. I will show you how to fully integrate this and any other belief statement you are not 100% aligned with in the next section. For now, though, simply make a note that you need to integrate this statement, and then go back and muscle test for all the other belief statements in the list above.
5. Go through the entire list and muscle test each statement. The ones that test strong ask: 'This belief is integrated at 100%.' Make a note of any beliefs that you test weak on.

Part Four: Belief Integration

Pick a belief from the list that you tested weak for. (In the unlikely case that you had no weak responses go to Appendix C, where there are over 150 belief statements, and test yourself on some of them that you are curious about. Test until you find one you test weak on. We all have them!) For illustration purposes, I will use the 'I love myself unconditionally' belief as an example of how to fully integrate a belief. Let me walk you through the steps before you actually do the exercise:

1. To begin, you will think of a situation that evokes strong feelings of gratitude, love, caring or other positive emotions, such as holding your baby son or daughter, a day of your favourite holiday, your favourite outdoor sanctuary, someone you love, a magical moment in your life or the like. Really connect in with the emotional aspects of the experience and amplify these feelings throughout your whole body.

2. Then, sit in the Whole Brain Posture and close your eyes. (See Figures 10.3–10.6.) If moving into the posture disrupted your immersion in the positive feelings, take a moment to connect back in with them. Immerse your whole body in those feelings.

3. Smile! Well, smiling is optional, but belief change doesn't have to be serious work. It's a joyful empowerment. It should be relaxing, fun and easy. Besides, smiling increases the release of serotonin in your brain—the happy chemicals. Smiling also activates your zygomaticus major muscle, a muscle that is linked to your thymus gland, which is the 'school and factory' for your white blood cells, which are responsible for immune system strength. A very good reason to smile a lot!

4. Silently repeat the belief statement you are attempting to fully integrate. In our example, it's 'I love myself unconditionally'. Repeat the belief statement silently until you feel some sort of internal signal that your mind–body has integrated this new belief. This 'signal' can take any number of forms or feelings, such as a feeling that energy is moving within your body, visual impressions, memories, a deeper sense of relaxation, changes in your breathing, body movements or twitches. It's okay not to feel anything different as well—just wait until you feel intuitively that the belief is integrated. Generally, the signal will be quick, often within 30 seconds of assuming the posture. Saturate yourself with these positive feelings as you repeat the belief statement silently. When you feel complete, open your eyes, come out of the Whole Brain Posture and take a natural deep breath.

You have now completed the integration process and you will now recheck that the belief is fully integrated using the muscle test.

The Whole Brain Posture

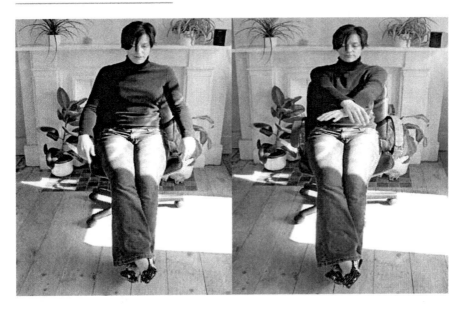

Figure 10.3 *Sit feet crossed (it doesn't matter which foot is on top).*

Figure 10.4 *Cross one arm over the other arm (it doesn't matter which arm is on top).*

Figure 10.5 *Bring your clasped palms up to your middle chest/heart area.*

Figure 10.6 *The full Whole Brain Posture.*

Part Five: Confirming the Belief-Change Process is Complete

The last step in the belief-change process is to 'post-test' the belief statement, making sure that the full integration into your subconscious was a success.

1. Stand in the muscle testing posture and speak the belief statement out loud. In this case, it is 'I love myself unconditionally'.
2. Your partner says 'Hold' and then muscle tests. You should test strong.
3. Raise your arm again, and as a double check, you say aloud, 'This belief is integrated at 100%.'
4. Your partner says 'Hold' and muscle tests you.

Almost all of the time, you will test very strong for the belief statement now. However, you may still test weak. That happens rarely, but it does happen, and is usually a sign that you came out of the Whole Brain Posture too soon. If you do test weak, resume the Whole Brain Posture and repeat the steps for fully integrating a belief and then the steps above for confirming the integration of the belief statement. You should now test strong. Your subconscious mind now holds this belief as a truth. Congratulate yourself!

The Gamma Belief Change Technique in Brief

1. Muscle test name and false name and pleasant and stressful experiences.

If muscle test is clear move to no. 2; if not, tap the ten meridian points then retest.

2. Muscle test belief statement.
3. If the muscle test is strong, also muscle test 'This belief is integrated at 100%.' Any weak statements, move to step 4.
4. Activate heart-based feelings of love, care and gratitude and immerse yourself in these feelings.

5. Move into the Whole Brain Posture.
6. Silently repeat the belief statement until you feel an internal 'signal' that it is integrated.
7. Post muscle test the belief statement.
8. Check it is integrated at 100%—'This belief is integrated at 100%.' If the test is strong you are complete.
9. If still weak, go back into the Whole Brain Posture and repeat steps 4–8.

Why This Works - The Gamma Breakthrough

When I measured subjects brain activity using an E.E.G during a belief change process, you see high levels of the gamma brain wave in the frontal lobes of the brain. This is followed by high levels of theta and alpha with a low level of beta brain wave activity.

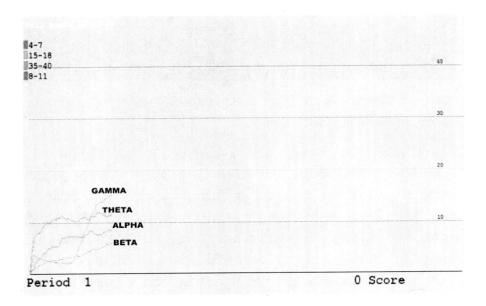

Figure 10.6 *Within as little as 60 seconds of deep immersion in this technique there is a huge level of gamma brain-wave activity in the frontal lobes. This is followed by high levels of theta and alpha and a low level of beta. The more activity you create in the frontal lobes, the less impulsive and reactive you are and the more potential you can express.*

This is a brain in a peak state of consciousness. This is the ideal state where you program your mind-body with new information and also receive new information through expanded awareness and higher level thought. New beliefs are mapped and patterned as a set of new 'electrochemical' connections which allow you to create new ways of thinking, new behaviours, and express new levels of potential.

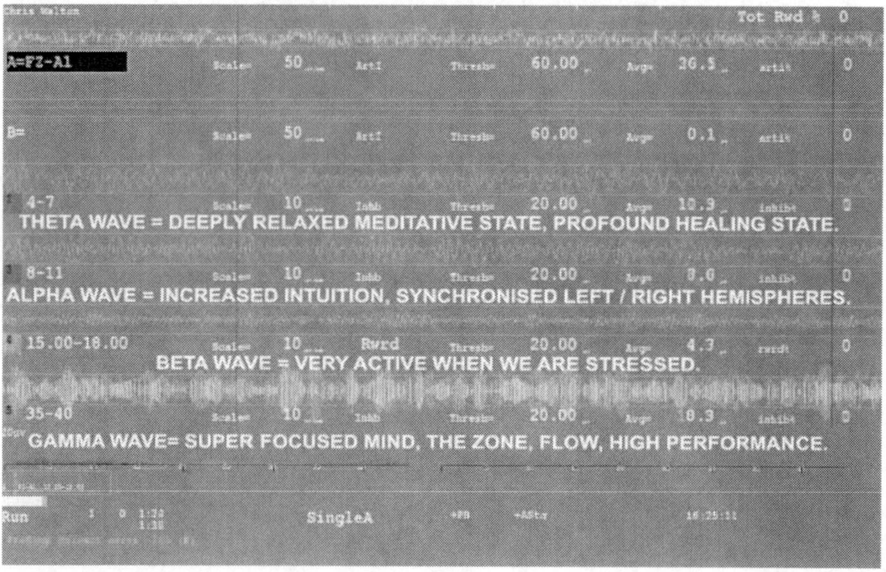

Figure 10.7 *Gamma is the brain wave on the bottom of the image, you can see it is the most active predominant brain wave.*

The 'whole brain posture' was devised by Dr Paul Dennison. It is an effective and simple way to use your body to help facilitate the alignment of the left and right hemispheres of your brain, so that they better communicate with one another. The right hemisphere controls the left motor functions of the body and vice-versa, by crossing your arms and legs at the midline of your body, you ensure that you are activating both hemispheres and creating what's termed a 'whole-brain' state. With the eyes closed, this posture very quickly creates a high level of alpha brain wave activity. This relaxes the body and leads to heightened levels of intuition, creativity, focus and an optimal balance between intelligence and logic and wisdom and insight.

Your heart is your body's main electrical power centre, producing 40–60 times more power than your brain. Remember from chapter 6 that your heart and brain are constantly sending signals to each other and that feelings of gratitude, happiness, appreciation, love, kindness etc., directly activate your brains frontal lobes, the most evolved part of your brain. The frontal lobes are like the symphony leader that quietens down the areas of the brain to do with bodily sensations and the emotional reactive centres. In this peak brain state, silently repeating the belief statement with intention creates electrical activity in the brain, influencing the body's chemical output and sending the information throughout and beyond the entire body. Your heart's huge power source is the carrier wave of the new information program—the new belief—that you are broadcasting into your body, amplifying that energy so that it reaches every cell of your body with each heartbeat. As Professor William Tiller says,

"When applied intentionality is focused through the heart into the daily life process, a greater rate of structural refinement occurs and thus the more rapidly does one's consciousness expand."[6]

Integrating a new belief program into the brain is rather like downloading a new piece of software into your computer. In a computer, there are a specific set of pathways dedicated to routing the information to the proper place in the hard drive's memory chips. Once the information is loaded, you can easily access it by simply clicking an icon. In your mind and body a similar process occurs. Your new belief is loaded into your subconscious mind, held there once it is fully integrated, and then is ready for you to access in your daily life – opening the way for new, inspired and self-empowering actions and behaviours. You can create new brain patterns for every area of your life.

I have called the **Gamma Belief Change Technique** without the muscle test the **Gamma Brain Technique**© and you can use it in four ways.

1. To program your subconscious mind with new beliefs and information. Simply repeat steps 4-6.

2. To achieve a heightened state of awareness and focus. Repeat steps 4 and 5.

You can use this technique to prepare yourself for a meeting, presentation, important/difficult conversation, to be calm, centred and present or anytime you need to de-stress and move into balance and a super focused mind state.

3. Problem Solving. Repeat steps 4 and 5.

When you have a problem and you need some clarity on what to do, do the following; a) Be very clear on your problem and intend to get some clarity on a solution and the best way to proceed. b) When you are deeply relaxed and your mind is calm, ask, "How can I solve this situation?" What do I need to do for the best outcome for all?" and other relevant questions. Remain relaxed and just experience what pops into your mind. Remember you are putting your brain into a peak functioning state. I suggest having a notepad and pen close by when you do this as often your brain will 'serve up' ideas and answers whilst in this deep state of relaxation. Answers and ideas also pop into your mind after completion of the technique when you are thinking about something else entirely.

4. Healing Meditation. Repeat steps 4 and 5.

Just 5-10 minutes of this technique as a meditation creates a profound sense of physical, mental and emotional relaxation and rejuvenation. The only goal here is to relax.

By using the Gamma Belief Change Technique and the Gamma Brain Technique©, you are unleashing the power of your beliefs to totally remake your life. If you integrate just two empowering beliefs a day—replacing out-dated and self-limiting ones with more life-affirming ones—you will have 60 new beliefs programs running within a month, affecting every thought, feeling, intention and action. How these new beliefs express themselves in your increased levels of success, health, wealth, love and happiness is up to you. What is it you truly want to change in your life? Where are you being held back or holding yourself back? No matter what question you ask, you will be brought back to a belief that is causing the manifestation of the experiences in your life. Change your beliefs, change your life!

Part Six: Creating Your Own Belief Statements

In Appendix C I have listed over 150 belief statements relating to:
❏ Change
❏ Self-esteem
❏ Relationships
❏ Prosperity
❏ Health and body
❏ Self-empowerment
❏ Effective communication
❏ Spirituality

These belief statements are exceptionally empowering and have been well tested on thousands of people. However, they are my words from my mind. Your belief statements may be different. A belief statement has to really 'resonate' with you, so now I will teach you how to write your own belief statements.

Creating and integrating your own belief statements are an essential part of the belief-change process and important in your success at repatterning your subconscious mind. Here are the guidelines for creating them:

❑ The more specific you are in the wording of your belief statements, the more effective they are.

❑ Use the first person. (Make 'I' statements.)

❑ Use the present tense. Only our conscious minds recognise time,as in past, present and future. The subconscious is always in the 'now'. So start your belief statements with phrases such as:

  • I do

  • I am

  • It is safe for me to

(See Appendix B for belief statement creation templates.)

Use positive wording about what will be true for you. As the famous psychiatrist Dr John Diamond says in his book *Life Energy and Emotions*, 'It is not the absence of the negative we want but the presence of the positive.'[7] For example, instead of writing 'I am not depressed', reword your belief statement as 'I am upbeat and hopeful'.

❑ Keep your belief statements short, sweet and juicy, meaning that when you say it to yourself, the statement really resonates and makes you feel good.

❑ Create statements for all areas of your life and every goal and desire you want to achieve or attain.

I cannot stress this last point strongly enough—nothing is off limits to the belief-change process, so go for it! In one of my workshops, a woman explained that she had been taking singing lessons for more than two years and had never been able to hit the note E. She created a belief statement around the goal of achieving this and fully integrated it during the workshop. Two days later she emailed me telling me that she had sung an E at her next singing lesson, much to her delight and that of her singing teacher.

When I began writing the first draft of this book, I constructed several belief statements for this project, such as 'All parts of me are ready, willing and able to write a book now'. That is a well-constructed belief statement, but it didn't have the emotional oomph I wanted, so I rewrote it, adding some juicy words. My revision was, 'All parts of me are ready, willing and able to write a best-selling book with ease and joy'. Now that's more like it! So follow this advice and make sure you add some powerful adjectives and adverbs to your own belief statements, really making them shine emotionally. Here are a couple of powerful statements as examples: 'I complete my projects with enthusiasm and satisfaction.' 'Choosing healthy foods increases my life energy and vitality.' 'I build harmonious relationships with ease and joy.'

As I said previously, if you integrate just two new belief statements per day, you are empowering yourself with 60 expansive and life-affirming beliefs per month. That's an exceptionally powerful new set of frequencies that you are broadcasting out into your world. When you plant seeds in your garden and you nurture and care for the newly sprouted plants, they will flourish. You don't go out every day to check the seeds to make sure they are growing. You simply know that with the right attention the seeds will germinate and grow into lush flowering plants. Gardening is an appropriate metaphor for the belief-change process. When integrating new beliefs into your mind–body system, sometimes the new beliefs blossom rapidly, in showy ways that get your attention; but others take time and have less ostentatious blossoms.

Although some people are very self-aware of their internal processes, most of us are not. We just don't have the practice of touching in and feeling what's going on deep inside of us. As you increase your awareness to how you feel day to day—and of how your reactions and choices are different from what they used to be—you will see the belief-change process in action. Each of us 'links' to the belief-change process in our own way, so it's difficult to make sweeping declarations about it. We are dealing with our subconscious mind, after all, and by its very nature it is not easily probed by conscious analysis. We learn about our subconscious beliefs by the evidence of our life—its condition in terms of emotional state, challenges and opportunities, positive and negative patterns. As you integrate new beliefs, pay attention to the subtleties of your life and watch for how small changes can lead to big effects over time.

Remember, you can 'upgrade' your belief program at any time, so make adjustments to your beliefs whenever you feel they are needed. Also remember the Emotional Balance Technique in Chapter 7, which you can use to discharge emotional stress. It's an extremely valuable and important technique that works in unison with the belief-change process.

A Reminder of What Beliefs Are

I'll end this chapter by revisiting the meaning of beliefs and sharing some stories from some of my clients and workshop participants. More testimonials are in Appendix D. I trust they will inspire you to begin the belief-change process immediately for yourself.

Beliefs are our filters of reality. They create our perceptions, and they are expressions of our potential. They are what shape our behaviours and actions. We can use the belief-change process to hone and fine-tune our beliefs. I already shared how I worked with my beliefs about writing this book. But I did not just focus on one belief. I worked with many of the nuances of the central belief about my ability to write this book. For example, some of the belief statements I worked with included:

❑ I enjoy the process of writing my book.

❏ I write my book with clarity and confidence.
❏ I deserve to write an inspiring book.
❏ I am inspired when writing my book.
❏ I am disciplined and patient when writing my book.
❏ It is easy and fun to write my book.

As you can see, I wanted to ensure that I had no hidden resistance at a subconscious level about writing. Yet, even with my beliefs in alignment with my goals, I had to take action, as obviously the book would not write itself. That's what our beliefs do—inspire us to act and create our life the way we want it, not the way we were doing it before. Interestingly, as I began writing this book, I found that working from my home office was not productive. I had a workshop coming up in Slovenia, so I decided to stay on for a week after teaching the workshop to write there. While in Slovenia, I had an intuition to test another belief: 'All parts of me are ready, willing and able to complete the first draft of my book in Slovenia now.' To my surprise, I tested weak. Now, if I were to try and work out why I held that belief, I might have been in Slovenia for months. I knew it didn't really matter why I held the belief, only that I did hold it, which was causing stress in my mind and body. So I worked with the integration process and Whole Brain Posture until I had fully integrated that belief. I ended up having an enjoyable and productive seven days of writing.

Very general belief statements, such as 'I love myself unconditionally', will have an effect on everything you do. One woman I worked with told me that the week following our private coaching session in which we worked with integrating this belief and others on self-esteem, she looked in the mirror and thought how pretty she looked. She was startled, as this was the first time she could remember thinking this about herself.

Beliefs can also reverberate through our lives in more expansive ways than we intended. One participant in a workshop I gave worked to integrate beliefs about sleep. She found that changing her beliefs in this area affected other behaviours and desires in unexpected ways. She emailed me:

Hi Chris

I'm still experiencing relatively big changes, which is astounding, given that it's only Tuesday morning! I guess being a massage therapist makes me absorb things like a sponge! Since Saturday night, I've been sleeping very deeply (to the point of being in a coma!), something I've not achieved for a good six months. I've suddenly started craving very healthy food, which may be a knock-on effect of the good sleep—no need for sugar/caffeine to keep me going all day. My shopping trolley in Tesco this morning was devoid of the usual ready meals; in fact, my stomach turned at the sight of them on the shelves! I've also suddenly become assertive—my parents say my voice is so much stronger on the phone. I've realised that clients and certain friends have been taking the mickey and it's been a total pleasure not behaving like a doormat. I'm not being rude or aggressive— let's just say I've been 'batting the balls back over the net'. It's caused a lot of confusion, but I know the dust will settle once they appreciate the boundaries I'm setting. This is so empowering. Thanks a million.

Bobbie

If you are not seeing the changes you want to, there are a few reasons that might explain why:

1. You have not been specific enough in your belief statements.
2. You need to change your belief statement, perhaps being more creative and touching in emotionally with how you word it. Remember, make it juicy!
3. You have not taken any action. Sitting at home waiting for things to happen is not going to express the life potential of your new belief programs. Changing your beliefs is all about being able to take new kinds of action, with a new attitude and a more positive outlook.

4. Your action has to be in the realm of possibility. This doesn't mean it's not daring or even outrageous, but it does have to be backed by realistic expectations. For example, I could integrate the belief that 'all parts of me are ready, willing and able to run the London marathon now', but if I don't start training for the marathon I probably am not ever going even to attempt to run it.

5. Aspects of your life actually are changing, but you are not aware of them. Remember, a changed belief is still a subconscious program. It's just a new one. Change can be subtle, and you might have to pay attention.

6. There might be an emotional energy block that is stopping you from taking action. Use the Emotional Balance Technique to eliminate this block.

Changing your beliefs and clearing your autopilot negative emotional reactions form the most empowering and life-enhancing personal growth process you can undertake. Create your own very specific goal-related beliefs and clear any emotional energy that feels 'out of sync' with your goals. Set a goal of doing a one-hour session each week with a partner or a group of friends and get motivated and inspired about expanding who you are and what you can achieve. Make time for feedback each week with your partner or group and support each other in creating the life that you want. Increase your awareness of synchronistic events in your life as you change your personal energy signature. You have an immense amount of power and potential waiting to be unlocked.

You have now learned a quick, easy and effective way to make deep and lasting changes in your life. The belief-change process is subtle in its practice, but its results can cause huge positive ripples of change in the quality of your life. In the last chapter the final question I ask you to consider is: 'How big do you really want to be?'

Key Points

- ❏ Energy psychology is based on the new scientific paradigm of change.
- ❏ Mind–body kinesiology is a direct bio-feedback interface with the subconscious mind.
- ❏ The heart's electromagnetic field imprints the information of the new belief to every cell of the body.
- ❏ You can change a belief you have had for a lifetime in one or two minutes.

11

THE MOST POWERFUL BELIEF YOU WILL EVER CHANGE

Our decade of research on transformation has found that dramatic and lasting change for the better springs from radically shifting your perception of who you are.

Dr Marilyn Mandala Schlitz

Who are you? That is one of the most profound questions we can ask ourselves, and yet most of us don't know how to answer it deeply or truly. We answer in terms of our relationship status—mother, father, son, daughter, husband, wife—or in terms of our job or professional status, or some other important but ultimately superficial role at our personality level. We rarely dare to go deeper. Yet the most powerful belief you will ever change arises from the question of who you think you are. Who are you and what is your potential as a human being? Quite simply, 'How big do you want to be?'

To answer that question, you have to delve much deeper than your personality level, which is simply one layer of who you really are. The word 'personality' derives from the Latin word *persona*, which means 'mask'. The study of personality is partly an examination of the masks that we wear—the many faces we show to the world according to the context in which we find ourselves. Your role/mask as a mother or wife is different than as an executive at your company. Your role/mask as a father is different than it is as a golf partner. All of these masks and roles arise from our inner psychological experience, which we collectively call our 'self'.

But what is the self? Ah, there's a question. Science tells us that 98% of all the atoms that make up the cells in our body are replaced within one year:

❑ Every five days, your stomach lining has completely replaced itself.

❑ Every thirty days, your skin is completely regenerated from new cells.

❑ Every six weeks you have an entirely new liver.

❑ Every six weeks, the raw material of your DNA is replaced.

❑ Within one year all of your brain cells have been recycled into new ones.

❑ In less than four years, your entire body has been remade down to the last atom.

So, who is this stable 'self' we all feel we have? As you now know from reading this book, you are a unique pattern of energy and information that shows up in the 'real' physical world as a mind and body of more than 50 trillion cells. With the birth of quantum physics and the realisation that the atom is not solid, we have all been asked to view ourselves with new eyes. We are dynamic beings made of energy. As physicist and author Frijof Capra succinctly explains,

> *Subatomic particles and all matter made from them, including our cells, tissues and bodies, are in fact patterns of activity rather than things.*[1]

As we move up the scale of awareness and understanding, we move from being the activity of our bodies, to that of our minds, to that of our spirits. All three together influence the quality of our lives. Cell biologist Bruce Lipton reminds us that as human beings, 'We are broadcast devices giving the field shape.'[2] As you make belief changes, the shape of your bio-field changes, affecting every aspect of your life from your DNA to the day-to-day experiences you attract. So, your belief about how 'big' you dare to be is profound, for the only limits to the shape and quality of your field and there-fore your life are the ones you place on it.

In his 1944 classic book *The Perennial Philosophy*, Aldous Huxley describes many levels of reality, with consciousness being the fundamental building block of the universe. He describes the universe as being more like a great thought than a great machine. As human beings, he says, we can access the entirety of the universe—and play in the field of infinite possibilities—through our consciousness, which is our non-local mind, the mind that is interconnected through the vast web of being with everyone and everything else. Talk about a grand vision of being!

Your personality self is localised in your social roles and played out through your material body. But there is an 'I' that is bigger than that, that is universal in its nature, and it is non-local and immaterial. The perennial philosophy teaches that our life's purpose is to become one with the universal, non-local consciousness of which we are a part in our truest nature. Our ultimate task as a human being is to fully awaken to our grandeur—to become one with the divine intelligence and then to help others to do the same. If you think I am sounding overly philosophical, let me bring the discussion back to science. At the frontiers of science, the view of our universe is literally mind-blowing. Consider the following three statements by leading-edge scientists:

❑ One of the fathers of quantum physics, Max Planck, said: 'We must assume behind this force in the atom is the existence of a conscious and intelligent mind. This mind is the matrix of all matter.'[3]
❑ Physics and astronomy professor Richard Conn Henry, from Johns Hopkins University in Baltimore, Maryland, wrote, 'The universe is made of energy and it is mental and spiritual in its nature.'[4]
❑ Medical doctor and author Deepak Chopra eloquently says, 'We are not physical machines that have learned to think, we are impulses of intelligence that have created the physical body.'[5]

The truth of the new science is that we are not biochemical machines controlled by genes and DNA. We are beings of energy and information, with an infinite potential.

Believing in ourselves according to this new scientific vision is a real stretch for most people. Yet the belief-change process is perfect for helping expand us to these daring new levels of being.

That's why I ask you to spend some time asking yourself, 'Who am I?' and 'How big do I want to be?' You can use the Emotional Balance Technique© and the Gamma Belief-Change Technique to make significant, empowering changes in all aspects of your life. And you can use it to blow the lid off any limitations you believe about yourself. Are you ready to do that?

Expanded States of Consciousness

How big can you be? I want to leave you with a message of exceptional hope and excitement for what is possible for you—and for your world. You can be as big as you choose to be—as big as you believe you can be. But getting there—to your grand self— usually takes a series of small steps. In this final chapter of the book, I will suggest some of the tried and true 'small steps' that have led people—across cultures and throughout time—to the attainment of lives that exceeded all their initial expectations. The first small step is to reacquaint yourself with who you really are. That means thinking about your own state of consciousness. Our ordinary waking state of consciousness is only one of many kinds of consciousness states we can access. We perceive our reality mostly based on what we are able to detect with our sense organs, so our reality is limited both by this physical constraint and by what is 'socially acceptable'. Not many of us want to stray too far outside the box of our social community. Yet being really, really big may mean that you have to stretch yourself more than a little outside that box. In Appendix A I will take you on a journey far outside that box, but here, in this chapter, we will stray only a little way beyond its confines.

Beyond waking consciousness are many other states of awareness. Some of the other states of consciousness include sleep,dreaming, meditation, daydreaming, ecstatic states, spiritual in sights and the hypnotic state. Each is a distinct quality of consciousness, and each expands our awareness of ourselves and our world in different ways. Each also can serve as a portal to information that is not accessible to us in our everyday, activity-focused conscious state. As examples, when the great pianist Rachmaninoff experienced creative blocks, he used hypnosis to achieve an altered state from which he could once again get the creative juices flowing. As a direct consequence of one of these hypnosis sessions, he created his world-famous Piano Concerto Number 2. He even dedicated it to his psychologist, Nikolai Dahl.[6]

The dreaming mind is also a doorway to insight, as physiologist Otto Loewi discovered. Early in his career, he had a hunch about how chemicals assisted in the transmission of nerve impulses. He ultimately put the idea aside when he could not think of an experiment by which he could test his hypothesis. Some years later, however, he had a dream in which the perfect experiment presented itself. He carried it out, proving his theory and ultimately winning the Nobel Prize for this work.[7] The physicist Niels Bohr, a father of quantum theory, got his model of the atom through a dream. He dreamed he was sitting on a sun of burning gas, with planets rushing past, hissing and spitting. They appeared to be connected to the sun by fine threads. Suddenly, as the gas sun solidified, the entire system of orbiting planets became motionless. At that moment, he woke up and knew that what he had seen was a metaphor for the correct model of the atom. He, too, was awarded the Nobel Prize for his work.[8]

Altered states of consciousness seem to tune the receiver wavelength of our brains and bodies to different frequencies than we can pick up with our normal waking consciousness. The great psychologist William James wrote,

Just as a primary wide-awake consciousness throws open our senses to the touch of things material, so it is logically conceivable that if they be higher spiritual agencies that can directly touch us, the psychological condition of their doing so might be our possession of a subconscious region which alone should yield access to them. The hubbub of the waking life might close a door which in the dreamy subliminal might remain ajar or open... if there be higher powers able to impress us, they may get access to us only through the subliminal door.[9]

The subliminal door is one that lies beneath the level of our normal, waking consciousness, and yet, paradoxically, when we access these deeper realms, we expand. We touch our 'transpersonal' self, as I explain below.

The Transpersonal Self

Institute of Noetic Sciences director Marilyn Mandala Schlitz and her co-authors write in their book *Living Deeply*,

> *Over our decade-long research program, we've found that one of the most common elements of consciousness transformation is an experience of the transpersonal: an experience in which consciousness or self-awareness extends beyond the boundaries of the individual personality... Transpersonal refers to a world view in which you see yourself as not just a separate individual ego, but as part of the greater whole.*[10]

To be all that you can be—to make really big changes in your life—you have to access the grandest part of yourself, your transpersonal self. Below are two of the small steps you can take to do so. Appendix A discusses more dramatic ways to access expanded states of consciousness. Of course, you can work to become more aware of your dreams and so access information they provide, and you can work with a hypnotherapist and use other kinds of insight techniques and tools. However, two of the easiest ways to access your transpersonal self are to cultivate your 'witnessing self' and to quieten your mind through meditation.

The Witnessing Self

When you think, you are aware that you are having thoughts. You can, in effect, observe and witness your thoughts and feelings. So who is this self that is doing the observing? It is the transpersonal self. The 'I' behind the 'i', so to speak. Some people call it the observer self, others the witnessing self. By simply cultivating an awareness of this larger I, you can access your deeper nature and change your life.

It's not as easy as it sounds to maintain a witnessing point of view. You have to continually take a 'time out' from your busy day and from the whirlwind thoughts of your 'monkey mind' to breathe, slow down and observe your mind. A very simple and powerful practice to enhance and strengthen your 'transpersonal self' is asking yourself just one question. As you go through your day experiencing a roller coaster of thoughts and feelings, rather than reacting to those thoughts and feelings, simply ask yourself: 'Who am I who notices these thoughts?' For example; if you are feeling frustrated, angry or impatient, just ask yourself 'Who am I who notices this frustration?'

By regularly asking yourself this question, you become less affected by your thoughts and feelings and begin to see them as a flow of information that you can observe. You are not your thoughts, you are not your feelings, you are not your body, you are the one who is able to observe and experience all of those things. After just a short while of cultivating your observer, you gain more control of your unresourceful autopilot subconscious reactions. By paying attention, you can stop, shift, change, and empower yourself in new and healthier ways. Then you can come back later and use the Emotional Balance Technique to any areas of your life where you have strong stress reactions. You can use the Gamma Belief Change Technique to test your beliefs about your observations and change them if need be. With practice, your witnessing self will always be active, running in the background of your mind like the operating system software runs in the background of your computer. You will be able to go about your normal routine but always be in a witnessing—or mindfulness—mode, checking on your state of being and heightening your level of self-awareness. When you are more self-aware, you have greater control over your responses, actions, thoughts and feelings. You become changed. You live the 'bigger' you by becoming conscious of how your daily life is being run on automatic pilot and then taking back the controls—and setting yourself free.

Meditation

Meditation is simply a method of relaxation. It does not have to be attached to any ritual or spiritual belief system. Staring at a gorgeous sunset can be meditative; being totally present in the moment is meditative. The basic requirement of achieving a meditative state is focused awareness. This slowing down, this turning inward, has been shown to affect the body in many healthful ways, from reducing stress to lowering blood pressure to boosting the immune system. Meditation is really a time out that we all deserve to give ourselves if for no other reason than that it supports our well-being. However, it can also be a doorway to insight and increased self-awareness.

Gamma Meditation Exercise: Who Am I

Undertaking a meditation session with an intention, such as asking yourself the question 'Who am I?', is one of the most powerful self-development practices. The Indian sage Ramana Maharshi was quoted as saying:

What is the use of knowing about everything else when you do not yet know who you are? Men avoid this enquiry into the true Self, but what else is there so worthy to be undertaken?[11] According to him, the inquiry into this question leads directly into enlightenment. Well, I'm not sure about enlightenment, but this meditation will allow you to access your transpersonal self.

Perform the Gamma Brain Technique© as described in chapter 10. When your body is relaxed and you have activated the heart field bring your attention to your breath, sensing the air on your nostrils both on the inhalation and exhalation. Simply relax and follow your breath. After a couple of minutes, as you feel more deeply relaxed, silently ask yourself 'Who am I?' and then gently bring your awareness back to your breath. Every time your mind wanders, simply guide your attention back to your breath and heart field and ask the question again: 'Who am I?' You have nothing to achieve or accomplish, and no expectations. Just allow any information that comes through in answer to this question to arise effortlessly within. Also notice any feelings that arise in your body.

No matter how many times your mind wanders, simply guide it back to your breath and heart field and repeat the question: 'Who am I?' Soon you may find that you are feeling lighter, softer and more expansive. You may begin to lose a sense of the boundaries of yourself and your body. You may feel a deep peace and a more perceptive sense of knowing. Allow any answers to the question to flow through you. Do not attach to them. Just allow them. Let them pass through you.

When you are ready slowly open your eyes and regain a sense of yourself and your body, concluding the meditation session. You might want to take a few minutes to write down any information you got in your meditation. Don't expect to remember it later. It's always best to write it down while the information is fresh in your memory.

So, How Big Do You Want to Be?

Our mind and our belief systems can be either bridges or barriers to expressing our highest potential. Updating our beliefs about who and what we are is an absolute necessity to increase our personal and collective peace, health and happiness. The techniques in this book provide an easy, quick and very effective way for you to expand your conception of yourself and to enhance every aspect of your life. You hold the key to the unfolding of your dreams, hopes and desires. My wish is that you will use this key wisely to unlock the hidden potential within you.

I also urge you to use what you have learned to contribute to the greater good. Each of us affects the world in our own small ways. We live in a non-local, interconnected universe, and we truly cannot know how our thoughts and actions will reverberate throughout the web of the universal mind. When we fully realise and embrace the truth that the real you, the you at your essence, is a field of pure, unbounded consciousness experiencing itself through a physical body, our world will be a very different place. As we love ourselves more, as we embrace our 'bigness' in more authentic ways, as we develop our transpersonal self we realise we are masterful creators. We can create a world of harmony where abundance is our natural birthright. We can relax, live and let live, be full of joy and concentrate on finding, and living, our own bliss. Now that sounds like the world in which I want to live! How about you?

APPENDIX A

DISCOVERING HOW BIG YOU CAN BE

In the last chapter, I asked you: 'How big do you want to be?' Here I will take you to places you might not have considered going—expanding your consciousness to experience a cosmic you. Quantum physics tells us we are all interconnected, with each other and with the very fabric of the universe. In a sense, we live in a participatory universe, where our conscious awareness brings reality into existence. If your reality seems small, then there are various ways you can expand your sense of self.

For millennia, people from cultures all around the globe have explored states of consciousness beyond waking, dreaming and meditative states. And so can you. These expanded states of consciousness provide you with access to knowledge and information that would not normally be available to you in your everyday awareness. These states can have a profound effect on who and what you think you are. In expanded states, you may dissolve the physical and perceptual boundaries of your ego self to realise you are much more than just a personality and a physical body. You can experience a deep connection and oneness with others and with nature.

Some of the greatest minds of modern times have had epiphanies and deeply creative insights while in altered states of consciousness. For example, psychologist Carl Jung was very interested in psychic phenomena and dream work because of his own, and his patients', experiences with altered states. Archimedes, Newton and Einstein used expanded states of awareness for insight that provided information relevant to their scientific theories. Writers, poets, filmmakers and artists have used altered states to envision new possibilities, frames of reference and ways of translating the world in their work. The highly esteemed and visionary psychiatrist Stanislav Grof, and many other medical professionals, induced altered states in thousands of patients in a clinical environment using small doses of LSD, when it was legal to do so back in the 1950s and 1960s. These patients reported that their experiences were extremely effective in helping them reach deep into their emotions to heal issues that traditional psychotherapeutic methods had little effect on. Most patients also reported that their visionary experiences expanded and enhanced their consciousness, moving them from a materialistic and mechanistic frame of reference to a more holistic world view. Many reported having sacred and spiritual experiences that profoundly changed them.

Psychedelics even fostered many of the technological innovations that you use on a daily basis. For example, the co-founder of Apple Computers, Steve Jobs, says using LSD as an aid to his creative vision was one of the two or three most important influences in his life. His partner, Steve Wozniak, described in *Time* magazine how he got the first concept for Apple Computers during an LSD trip. Francis Crick, the Nobel Prize-winning father of modern genetics, was using LSD when he first had the idea of the double helix structure of DNA in 1953. Crick told fellow scientists that he often used LSD in small doses to boost his powers of thought and creativity.[1]

There are many ways of entering altered and expanded states of consciousness, such as through dreams, ecstatic music and dance, sacred sound, entheogens (psychedelics), sacred sexual practices, meditation, prayer, chanting, blissful scenery, intense sports performance and even hysterical laughter. Altered states of consciousness seem to tune the receiver wavelength of the brain and body to different frequencies, allowing you access to a wider scope of information than is normally available and to new ways of perceiving and knowing the world and yourself.

I will share with you three ways you can expand your awareness, using my own life and experiences as examples. There are many other ways. I want to be clear that I am not advocating the use of psychedelics or any of the other modalities I describe below. If you choose to use any of them, you should do so only after fully educating yourself and under the supervision of someone experienced in that modality.

Out-of-Body Experiences—My Experience

Researching expanded states of consciousness has been a deep interest of mine for many years. The first time I went to the Monroe Institute in Virginia was in 2000, after I heard a friend of mine explain that using its techniques helped you experience how 'you are more than your physical body'. So I went off to a six-day retreat. As I mentioned in Chapter 5, the Monroe Institute has a patented sound technology called Hemi-Sync® that enhances awareness and consciousness. Each participant goes into a private sound-proofed booth called a CHEC unit (which stands for controlled holistic environment chamber) for between four and six hours a day and uses the Hemi-Sync technology, which sends different frequencies into each ear, frequencies that are masked by either pleasant music or a guided meditative journey. The two different sounds alter your brain waves and thus your state of consciousness. For each session, you have a theme and set an intention, such as to retrieve early memories, heal a past wound, access heightened creativity and the like.

My experiences were dramatic. I felt my sense of self expand and my consciousness enlarge and shift, such that I had access to information and thoughts—which would just pop spontaneously into my mind—that I had never had before and never imagined having. In a few sessions I felt I healed some emotional childhood wounds, accessed buried childhood memories, and generally came to realisations and understandings of my current unresourceful behavioural patterns. In other sessions I experienced a magnification of 'self', feeling a huge expansion in which I was connected to everyone in my life in a new and deeper way, and to everything in nature and in the cosmos. The boundaries of myself evaporated and I experienced a profound unity of consciousness. After a few days of undertaking these sessions, I was feeling extremely relaxed and calm. I felt an exquisite sense of inner peace and happiness. I felt I had touched my true nature and essence. After about 15 sessions, I was flying! This sense of unboundedness felt nothing like a caffeine or adrenaline high—I simply felt filled with light and freedom.

In one of my last sessions, I felt myself going very deep within, losing all sense of my physical boundaries. I'm not sure how much time passed, but suddenly I realised that I was above my body looking down on it. I was observing myself reclining on the bed in the CHEC unit, yet my consciousness was freed from my body. This felt nothing like a dream or my imagination. The consciousness of the 'me' that was looking down was far more real than the 'me' on the bed. I know this sounds bizarre and possibly very hard to believe, yet there I was, out of my body and still fully conscious and aware, seeing my physical body in all its details. Everything felt natural and in order. Nothing felt strange. Yet after a while, I seemed to 'wake up' to what was happening, and I felt a surge of shock and fear. As soon as I did, I shot back into my physical body with a jolt. It felt like I had been dropped as a dead weight from a two-foot height. I cannot tell you in words what the next moments were like as I tried to piece together what had happened. It was very clear that it was not a dream. I knew that in some way I was more than merely a physical body and had just experienced being what I am in my essence—an unbounded spirit. That realisation really shook me up and the entire experience changed my view of reality. Talk about a change of belief!

You don't have to use the Monroe Institute technology or methodology to initiate an out-of-body experience. There are many books by people who claim to know how to induce them at will. You can explore these if you are interested. You won't be alone in doing so. As renowned consciousness researcher and psychologist Professor Charles Tart explains, thousands, if not millions, of people alive today have had the experience of existing outside the space of their physical bodies for a brief period and experiencing this separate state as real, not as a dream or imaginary experience. Tart's research reveals that the experience is similar no matter what your background or belief system. A typical sequence of an out-of-body experience starts with the sudden feeling of being free from your physical body and is almost immediately followed by amazement. For many people, the amazement is quickly displaced by fear, and they tend to pop back into their body as a consequence. So practice is required to acquaint yourself with the unique perceptions, and to allow yourself some time to get used to the feelings and to learn to control your movements while out of the body.

What can you do while you are out of your body? Just about anything! You can travel beyond the speed of light, thinking yourself someplace else. You can explore the cosmos. You can focus on acquiring insight and creative vision. For example, Tart reported on a woman who claimed she regularly had out-of-body experiences while sleeping and dreaming, and during this time out of her body she was able to gain useful information. To test her claim, Tart wrote a five-digit number on a piece of paper and placed it on a ledge, high on a wall near the ceiling, where the only way to read the number would be from above it. After a few nights the woman reported that she had left her body and floated to the ceiling and read the number 38957. She was correct.

Tart's colleague, psychologist Professor Stanley Krippner, decided to repeat this experiment, only using a picture instead of a number. Using extremely tight scientific controls to prevent any kind of deception, his research team selected a number of famous art illustrations, and one was chosen at random in a way that prevented anyone from knowing which one was the 'target' picture.

The image was put into an envelope and placed on a ledge near the ceiling in the lab. A medical student who claimed he had out-of-body experiences while he slept was tasked to try to open the envelope and view the picture during one of his out-of-body flights. The student's brain waves were measured over a period of nights as he slept. On the fourth night, his brain showed an odd, slow brain-wave signature. When the student awakened, he reported having been out of his body. He said, 'I have just gone out of my body and seen the picture. It is a sunset.' When the researchers retrieved the envelope and opened it, the picture they pulled out was titled 'Memory of a Perfect Sunset'. The researchers worked out that the chances of dreaming of a sunset are approximately 1 in 50,000, so they were open to at least considering that the student had indeed left his body and viewed the picture or else had somehow paranormally acquired the information telepathically in a dream. Krippner concluded,

Here we have two experiments that indicate that even though mind and body are one, sometimes the mind takes a little vacation from the body, just like the body takes a little vacation from the mind and sometimes this does happen during dreams.[2]

Remote Viewing

Remote viewing is the ability to see things at a distance beyond the range of the normal senses.[3] You project your mind or awareness to a 'target' and are able to view that target just as if you were there physically. You also can report on your experiences while you are doing remote viewing. This is not so much an altered state of consciousness as much as an expanded state of awareness. And anyone can be trained to do it. Why bother? Because it shows just how 'unbounded' you truly are. Your mind is not confined to your brain or your skull. It can range throughout the world and even the cosmos, and you can be aware and in control the whole time. Unlike out-of-body experiences, remote viewing is more a technical skill than it is a spiritual or metaphysical experience. You don't feel that you have left your body, although your consciousness appears to be able to travel anywhere, so it does not induce fear or shock the way an out-of-body experience can.

The CIA conducted secret research on remote viewing for more than 25 years during the Cold War, trying to keep up with the Russians, who were far advanced in their study of remote viewing and the paranormal in general. Once the CIA programme was declassified about 15 years ago, many ex-military remote viewers began teaching this skill to the general public. You can now go through a training programme and learn how to 'send your mind' to distant places and retrieve verifiably accurate impressions and information about that place.

Let's back up a bit though. Even before the CIA got involved, two physicists, Russell Targ and Hal Puthoff, were exploring this technique, developing an understanding of it and how best to do it. They worked at the innovative Stanford Research Institute, where they pioneered the technique.

Eventually, they were called on to teach it to hundreds of military personnel in secret military and CIA remote viewing programmes. The original methodology was to have an 'agent' go out into the field to a random location, such as a park or local landmark, and simply observe the site in detail—its natural features, buildings, people, colours, shapes and so on. A subject in the lab would follow a specific series of steps to free his mind to go to the location. He would then write down or draw his impressions of the location. The subject was isolated from any possible means of knowing the agent's location, and yet many times he was able to describe it accurately, reporting that his awareness appeared to be at the site and he could see it in all its details, just as if he was there. A scientific review of 26,000 remote viewing sessions conducted between 1973 and 1988 revealed that the results were accurate to a hugely statistically significant degree, with odds against chance of a billion billion to one.[4]

I attended a remote viewing workshop in the US with physicist Russell Targ. As one of the developers of the technique, he had participated in some of the military exercises, serving as a coach to remote viewers. He reported that once he and the remote viewer he was working with sent their 'non-local mind' into the Kremlin and explored it at will for two hours. They recorded their impressions, and those notes were filed away. Years later, when the Cold War had ended and information was accessible from the Soviet Union, their impressions were verified as being highly accurate. Some people have even suggested that it was this remote viewing 'war' between the US and the USSR that brought an end to the Cold War, as both sides knew their secrets were no longer completely secure.

Remote viewing is certainly interesting, showing us that our minds are 'non-local', meaning they can be projected outside of our bodies and still function correctly, so that reliable information can be discerned and retrieved. Physicist Dr Claude Swanson writes in his book *The Synchronistic Universe*,

The remote viewing program teaches us several important lessons about the laws of the universe and our true abilities as

human beings. These new lessons pose a challenge to contemporary science and to our stereotypes of what a human being is. Remote viewing teaches us that we are more than our physical bodies. We have a consciousness which is not limited to our physical body, and can move seemingly anywhere in space and time and bring back information. These new aspects of human abilities and consciousness will lead to a revolution in science, and an expanded view of both science and ourselves.[5]

In the Amazon with the Shaman—My Experience with Ayahuasca

Every culture in human history has used some kind of natural consciousness-altering substance. They have used them to cement social relationships, divine the future, call for rain, find animals in the hunt, and expand vision to access the spiritual realms. However, the most common use is for healing. By altering consciousness, shamans claim to travel the inter-dimensional realms to detect what is wrong with a patient and to find a cure or a helpful remedy. These consciousness-altering plant ceremonies are still undertaken today in many parts of the world. In our culture, which shuns the use of consciousness-altering substances, natural or not, psychedelics are still used by the 'underground'. People from all walks of life and for a host of reasons find it useful to expand their consciousness using plant-derived natural psychedelics.

In parts of South America, the most common and powerful consciousness-expanding plant 'medicine' is ayahuasca, a large woody vine whose scientific name is *Banisteriopsis caapi*. It is made into a tea with another plant, often Chacruna. The two plants have to be boiled together to make the resulting 'tea', capable of inducing altered states of consciousness.

Over the years the use of ayahuasca has spread into the western world, and many travellers and seekers have ventured into the Amazon to participate in ayahuasca ceremonies. Ayahuasca has also been the subject of many scientific studies, with clear evidence showing that it increases brain cell growth (neurogenesis) and improves serotonin uptake, helping to relieve depression.[6] It is safe to use, but is not a pleasant experience, as the ayahuasca tea is bitter and generally tastes disagreeable. However, its effects can be spectacular. Most people report extremely heightened states of consciousness, access to 'spiritual' realms and a connection to the deepest aspects of nature that are not possible in normal waking states of consciousness.

In 2006, I went to Brazil to participate in a 17-day ayahuasca retreat, during which I would take part in six ayahuasca ceremonies. The setting was on the beautiful Bahia coast. We were a merry band of about 30 people from all walks of life and from all over the world. As I got to know these fellow adventurers, I learned that they shared a common motivation for attending the retreat, which was to heal themselves on all levels so that they could be happier, more peaceful and have a deeper understanding of who they really were.

After relaxing for the first day, we participated in the first ceremony on the second night. We gathered around and watched the shaman bless the ayahuasca—which shamans consider to be a plant spirit with a beingness all its own—and chant and commune with it in his own language. One at a time, we went up to the shaman to receive a cup of the ayahuasca brew. As we drank it, each of us thought of a specific intention for our inner journey. After we had all ingested the brew, we reclined under the palm trees, near a central fire pit.

The shaman then began singing special songs called *icaros*, which are sacred songs that guide the participants' energy, visions and healing during the ceremony. I had mixed feelings as I began this journey, feeling both relaxed and excited—and just a little bit nervous. I focused on the stars I could see shining though the palm trees, enjoying the warm night. Soon the fire, with its hypnotic flames, drew my attention. As I relaxed more deeply, the *icaros* seemed to be flowing through every part of my body. I allowed them to work their magic, and about an hour later, I began to feel huge waves of energy pulsating through my body. I felt as if I were being bathed in a warm, nurturing ocean. The waves seemed to be emanating from within me, but at the same time from far outside of me. It was an indescribable feeling, one I had never experienced before. A little while later, the energy waves became stronger, growing ever more intense, until they were overpoweringly strong. Suddenly I began vomiting and rolling around like I was a rag doll being tossed around by a playful dog. (It is not uncommon to vomit while journeying with ayahuasca, as it is a purgative.) I was defenceless against these waves of energy. I felt as if every cell in my body was riding huge wild rapids. My mind felt like I was on some giant rollercoaster, and I didn't know where the next turn or dip was going to be. My physical boundaries were dissolving into these waves of energy; I was losing my body and along with it any sense of who I was.

The next three hours were extremely challenging and cathartic, and are nearly impossible to describe accurately in words. I began seeing an incredible visual display of interconnectedness among all the trees and plants. Fibres of light radiated from them and everything else around me, so my entire visual experience became one of a huge matrix of interconnected spectrums of light. As I looked at the trees I realised that at the deepest level there was no separation between me and them. We were energetically connected by light. I looked at the other participants and realised that at this deepest level we were all integral parts of an interconnected, intelligent consciousness. My physical boundaries were no longer recognisable and my being continued to expand, until I merged into this vast matrix of energy, which was intertwined with a matrix of energy from every being, animal and plant on earth. The expansion continued further still, until I was part of a larger matrix of all the planets, solar systems, galaxies and star systems in the universe. And still it went on, beyond the known universe to regions unknown. I sensed an infinite multidimensional intelligence behind it all. There were systems within systems within systems, much like our DNA within our cells, which are within our organs and tissues, which are within our bodies, which are combined into societies, and those into countries, and those into the world, and on and on.

This was the most astonishing experience of my life. I became aware that consciousness is a field of infinite energy, information and intelligence—and I, as Chris Walton, was a droplet of that consciousness having a physical experience as Chris Walton, born into a material body on January 19, 1970. I understood that we all are consciousnesses born into physical bodies with the ultimate goal of realising our part in the whole and awakening to the experience of our true self. And I was not only human. I was the trees, insects, noises, wind, other people, songs, stars—my consciousness was the consciousness of everything. I was aware that the consciousness I access in day-to-day life is just a miniscule fraction of what is available to me—and to each of us. I was bathed in a supernatural ecstasy, in a state of cosmic unity of consciousness that continued for hours.

Some time later—time was not important to me—my individual mind started to reconstruct itself. I found myself trying to analyse my feelings and experience, trying to make sense of it all. I wanted to put it all in definable boxes and clear-cut categories. I witnessed my own process, detached from myself: the mind of Chris was trying to reduce the experience to separate parts so that his rational self could make sense of things and say, 'Ahh! This is what is happening, and it's okay.' My mind was struggling to frame a picture, and to make that picture into the 'real reality'. Yet almost as soon as this process started, I was blasted back out into the infinite pool of pure interconnected and expanded cosmic consciousness. This back-and-forth mind movement went on for hours: one moment I was rationally trying to define and categorise and the next I was in a state of pure cosmic unity. I finally came to see that I could learn from this see-sawing of my consciousness. It was like a lesson being taught me: we reduce the cosmic down to the mundane. That's what we do all of our lives, creating limitations through the conditioning of our minds and losing the reality of how huge and interconnected we really are with everyone and everything else in the cosmos.

After several more hours of this kind of rollercoaster experience, my mind settled down and I relaxed into a state of ecstatic bliss. I lay on the ground for hours, feeling this bliss and marvelling at my new understanding of what I am—and what we all truly are. We are without any doubt beings who have for some reason decided to materialise on planet Earth to become creators of our own destinies. We are here to experience the physical, yet our goal is to awaken and realise that we are far more than the physical. Every second of every day our beliefs, thoughts and feelings determine what we are and how we view ourselves. We have access to a state of being of pure loving awareness within an unlimited matrix of possibilities, and to engage this infinite field is our true destiny.

This single experience profoundly changed my life. From that moment on I have felt a deeper connection to nature and look at people with 'new eyes', knowing that at a core level of reality we are one. This was a brief account of one of the six ayahuasca ceremonies I participated in. They were all equally powerful, deeply insightful and healing on all levels of my being. Yet I learned that they were also larger than me. The shaman explained that in the ceremonies three levels of healing traditionally take place: our own personal healing, a collective group healing because we are all connected and our individual healing and intentions affect everyone else, and a global healing since we are all connected in the larger universal mind.

Ayahuasca is not for everyone. Sometimes the experiences can be frightening and extremely challenging. If you are the type of person who likes to keep your boundaries fixed and to stay within the status quo, then it's not for you. However, if you are open to dissolving your personal boundaries to explore more of who and what you are, then an ayahuasca journey can provide a direct and powerful means to that end. However, as the shamans say, you do not choose ayahuasca, it chooses you. It is a plant spirit that must be treated with respect, and it is best to wait until you 'feel its call' before exploring working with it.

★ ★ ★

No matter how you choose to expand your awareness, doing so can be a satisfying and even a life-changing experience. A transformative experience is, in the words of Dr Stanislav Grof, something that 'comes about when you are forced to reconcile your ordinary world view with insights gained from extraordinary or non-ordinary experiences.'[7] You now know that you are no ordinary being! And so, my question still stands, 'How big do you want to be?' It is up to you to answer that most important of questions for yourself.

APPENDIX B

TEMPLATES FOR BELIEF STATEMENTS

I now…

I am…

All parts of me are ready, willing and able to…

I deserve…

It is safe for me to…

It is easy for me to…

It is natural for me to…

It is my birthright to…

It is my god-given birthright to…

I'm so happy and grateful now that…

APPENDIX C

BELIEF STATEMENTS

B elow are over 150 empowering belief statements. Test yourself to see if you are alignment with them. You can choose the ones that are most applicable to the changes you want to make in your life now. Ultimately, being in alignment with them all will be tremendously empowering.

Belief Statements for Change

1. I can change.
2. It's safe for me to change.
3. I want to change.
4. It's easy for me to change.
5. I learn new things easily.
6. Change creates new opportunities for me.
7. Change means personal growth.

Belief Statements for Self-Esteem

1. I deeply accept and appreciate myself.
2. I forgive myself for all my imperfect thoughts and actions—past, present and future.
3. I love myself unconditionally.
4. I am worthy of being loved.
5. I love all parts of my body.
6. I accept my imperfections as opportunities to learn valuable lessons in my life.
7. I deserve to be happy.
8. I deserve the very best life has to offer.
9. I deserve to love myself.

10. I deserve to be loved by (input a specific name here or simply say 'by others').
11. I deserve to love (input a specific name here or simply say 'others').
12. I am patient and curious when others criticise me.
13. I am confident and self-assured about who I am.
14. I am confident and self-assured about my life.
15. I am the best me I can be in each moment.
16. I have faith and confidence in my future.
17. I trust myself.
18. I take responsibility for my own well-being.
19. I am proud of who I am.
20. I am at peace with myself now.

Belief Statements for Relationships

1. It's easy for me to give love to (input the name of a specific person or simply say 'others').
2. It's easy for me to receive love from (input the name of a specific person or simply say 'others').
3. I am worthy of an intimate, passionate, romantic relationship now.
4. I am willing to risk loving and being loved.
5. It is easy and natural for me to express my sexuality in a relationship.
6. I am able to maintain my individuality in my relationship (could name a specific person).
7. I release my relationship with (input a specific name) when it's time to 'let go'.
8. It's important for me to set boundaries in my relationships, and I do.
9. It is important for me to get my needs met in a relationship.
10. I am able to experience freedom in a relationship.
11. It's okay for my partner (input a specific name) to disagree with me.
12. I accept that my relationships change.
13. It's okay for me to express my truth in a relationship.

14. I allow others to grow and change or to stay as they are in a relationship.
15. I am true to my feelings in a relationship.
16. I allow myself to learn from others as they learn from me.
17. I allow myself to be sensitive and vulnerable in a relationship.
18. I allow others to learn their own lessons in a relationship.
19. I learn from my past relationships and create even better ones in the future.
20. I take full responsibility for my actions in my relationships.

Belief Statements for Prosperity

1. I trust myself to manage money honestly and sensibly.
2. Every part of me is ready, willing and able to create lots of money now.
3. I am calm and self-assured when I have money.
4. I am calm and self-assured when I do not have money.
5. I deserve to have all the money I need.
6. My worth as a person and my financial worth are two different things.
7. It's okay for me to want money.
8. I enjoy making lots of money.
9. I am confident and self-assured when I ask for business and for payment.
10. I receive and accept money with love and gratitude.
11. It's okay to have more money than I need.
12. It's okay for me to have more money than other people.
13. It's okay for me to make mistakes with money.
14. It's safe and appropriate for me to create lots of money.
15. Money is a wonderful tool that I use to create possibility for myself and others.
16. My world is a friendly place and willingly provides whatever I need.
17. I can make all the money I need doing a job that I love.
18. I can afford to take time off to rest and nurture myself whenever I need to.

19. I am proud of my work results and deserve my rewards.
20. Money is another manifestation of energy.

Beliefs about Your Body and Your Health

1. It is my natural birthright to be happy and healthy.
2. My mind and body system heals itself, naturally and quickly.
3. I choose to live a healthy and vibrant life.
4. I nurture my physical body in healthy and loving ways.
5. I accept optimal health as a natural part of my life.
6. I release all unnecessary stress from my body now.
7. My body is filled with peace and joy now.
8. The healing energy of love flows through every cell of my body now.
9. I am safe and calm during the healing process.
10. I lovingly release all causes of 'dis-ease' from my past.
11. Every day in every way, I am getting healthier.
12. My sleep is deep and relaxing and I awaken refreshed.
13. I have all the energy and focus I need to accomplish my goals and to fulfil my desires.
14. It's safe for me to be slim and healthy.
15. It's easy and fun for me to be slim and healthy.
16. It's safe and appropriate to change the shape and weight of my body.
17. I can be everything I want to be as a healthy and fit person.
18. I love and accept my body as it is and as it changes.
19. I see beauty in all parts of my body.
20. I enjoy taking care of myself physically, mentally and emotionally.

Beliefs about Self-Empowerment and Professional Development

1. I trust the decisions I make.
2. I trust the divine guidance I am receiving.
3. I acknowledge my abilities and responsibility to make a positive difference in the world.

4. I proactively embrace the opportunities that come with change.
5. I now take the initiative to create my life the way I want it.
6. I speak my personal truths with commitment, love and wisdom.
7. I learn and grow from my mistakes.
8. I use time efficiently and creatively and I experience having all the time I need.
9. My fears give me lessons that lead me to wisdom and power.
10. I take the risks necessary to live my life openly and honestly.
11. I enjoy making my life work.
12. I take full responsibility for myself.
13. I experience the potential in myself and others in all my life experiences.
14. I do what I love and love what I do.
15. I am assertive in meeting my own needs.
16. I take 100% responsibility for the results I create in my life.
17. I love my life.
18. I take action on my projects with inspiration and energy.
19. I embrace my uniqueness.
20. I create my own life with my thoughts, feelings and actions.
21. I now live life to the fullest.
22. I am grateful for my gifts and talents.
23. I use my talents to the greatest benefit for myself and others.
24. It is easy for me to do the work I love.
25. I am richly rewarded for doing the work I love now.

Beliefs about Effective Communication

1. I communicate my skills, knowledge and experience with clarity and confidence.
2. I listen to what others have to say with genuine interest.
3. I am a powerful and effective communicator.
4. I seek first to understand others before trying to be understood.
5. I am open and honest in my communication.
6. I let people finish talking without interrupting.

7. My opinions are as valid and important as anyone else's.
8. I understand that we all filter the world differently.
9. It's easy for me to agree to disagree.
10. It's okay for others to disagree with me.
11. I find it easy to give compliments to others.
12. I find it easy to receive compliments from others.
13. I trust my ability to say the right thing at the right time.
14. I give feedback with empathy and fairness.
15. I trust my ability to communicate effectively.
16. I can admit when I am wrong.
17. I am comfortable speaking to large groups of people.
18. People like to be around me.
19. I naturally look for the good in other people.
20. I am non-judgemental about others, and allow everyone to be who they are.

Beliefs about Non-locality and Spirituality

1. I am connected to everything and everywhere, past, present and future.
2. I am a spiritual being having a human experience.
3. I can easily access the field of infinite intelligence.
4. My true essence is pure consciousness experiencing itself.
5. I am all that is.
6. My goal in this life is to love myself and others.
7. I am pure, unbounded loving awareness.
8. I am whole, complete and connected in everything I do.
9. The universe is a multi-dimensional web of infinite intelligence and I am an integral part of it.
10. I am everything and everything is in me.
11. The universal Spirit provides me with all I need and desire.
12. My energy is clear and directed, so that I manifest whatever I choose easily.
13. My heart is open to myself and to others.
14. My heart is open to receiving the love of the universal Spirit now.
15. Universal intelligence flows through me.

16. When I am quiet and go within, all the answers I need are available to me.
17. The universe is a loving and positive place.
18. My life is a reflection of my spirit.
19. I am in touch with my deepest spiritual essence.
20. No matter what is happening around me, I choose peace.
21. I live by the Golden Rule that I do unto others as I would have them do unto me.
22. I easily accept that everyone has their own spiritual beliefs.
23. I am friendly and open with people whose beliefs differ from mine.
24. I am open to receive the blessings of others.
25. I am considerate of all creatures, for they are part of the web of life.

APPENDIX D

GAMMA BELIEF CHANGE TESTIMONIALS

'I've done a lot of work over the last 20 years in personal and professional development but the course that really made the difference was Chris's Gamma Healing Course. To be successful and live the life of our dreams we have to change our beliefs and this is exactly what Chris's course does. Chris's course has enabled me to become successful as an entrepreneur as well as an academic. I feel this course stands out from any other course and I would really recommend it to anyone to improve any area of their life and achieve their goals and perhaps to help others do the same.'

Vlatka Hlupic, Professor of Business and Management
University of Westminster, London

'I've been a GP for 35 years and a gestalt therapist for 20 years, I went on Chris's course and I have to say this particular way of working is completely life changing. It has changed my life so much so that I'm actually leaving medicine, taking up a new kind of role working with psychology and this kind of work I have learned in Chris's course. I've seen fundamental quick shifts in my own patients in general practice from giving up smoking to really deep profound shifts in confidence, self-esteem and self-worth. I feel like I have got onto a magic carpet and I'm really grateful to have completed Chris's courses.'

Dr Melanie Salmon, UK

'These techniques really create deep change.'

Kazadi Kalangu, M.D Brain Surgeon and Professor of Neurosurgery
Vice President of the World Federation of Neurosurgical Societies

'This book changed my life—literally! My crippling fear of public speaking has been holding me back all my life. Having completed the belief-change process around my fear, I am now shaping my future around teaching and public seminars. I urge you not to miss this opportunity to transform your life!'

Rhoda Kingston, BA, BSc, naturopath

'As a direct result of Chris's belief change processes I won the British Open Tournament beating the world no. 1 and achieved my career best no. 3 world ranking.'

Anthony Ricketts, professional squash player

'I experienced an increase in my self-esteem and sense of freedom. I worked with my clients and really saw a difference in their lives after applying the techniques I learned on Chris's course.'

Alan Zepec, executive coach, Croatia

'I had a block in my belief systems as to whether I was capable of leaving my job and starting a business on my own. The blocks were about the financial implications and lack of security compared to what I was used to after being in the same organisation for six years. After completion of the course I made the steps forward to create my new life and I have been ecstatically happy since doing so.'

Ivan Miljan, Croatia

'The next time I played after our session was, what I thought then, the best I have ever played. But after I just kept playing better, and on the last Tuesday night I played against a Oxfordshire men's county player and I won 9-7 in the fifth.

I have been feeling good on court and the main difference I have found, was the last couple of times I have played I have felt confident and not intimidated even if I was expected to lose comfortably, and even if my opponent was a lot bigger and stronger than I am.

All in all squash has been going fantastically since I saw you last. Thanks a lot.'

Alex, 14-year-old squash player

'The techniques I learned on Chris's course are the fastest and most effective techniques of change I have found in about 23 to 24 years of self-development work.'

Ivan, pilot, Bulgaria

'My wife has seen so many changes in me, and my career has improved tremendously since doing Chris's belief change courses.'

Dr Anthony Sawyer, GP, London

'After using the belief change techniques I had a new level of belief in every aspect of my next race. I came 2nd in my age group and it was quite simply a perfect race.'

Andy Brodziak, Iron Man triathlete

'The two-day workshop was life transforming. I noticed physical changes straight away.'

Stephanie B., natural health practitioner

'It's a brilliant, innovative and quick way to get people to make changes in their lives. I would strongly recommend it to anybody.'

Jenny D., owner, complementary health clinic, Somerset, UK

'I've used many techniques but these are the best tools I have used in 25 years of working as a management consultant and trainer.'

Ole Bloch, Denmark

'One of the biggest benefits of Chris's workshop was our being able to manifest our new healing centre. It helped with our ability and confidence to move our business forward.'

Dr Lilly and Russell, Brighton, UK

'Having done Chris's course my life has changed more than I could have imagined. I'm much more confident in my relationships, both personal and professional. The course was fascinating with great techniques and it 100% worked. I would highly recommend the course.'

Charlotte S., Reading, UK

'The course was so good I decided to sponsor the courses in my own country of Slovenia. The courses continue to exceed delegates' expectations.'

Marjana B., executive coach, Slovenia

APPENDIX E
TRAINING

Gamma Healing Workshops

Unique 1:1 Coaching

Energy, Resilience, Performance Corporate Training

www.ChrisWaltonUK.com

REFERENCES

Introduction

1. Adapted from Shane, www.Elite feet.com, December 2007.
2. Ernest Rossi, adapted from *The Psychobiology of Mind-Body Healing*, 1986.
3. Andrew Newberg, *Why We Believe What We Believe*, 2006.

Chapter 1

1. Andrew Newberg, *Why We Believe What We Believe*, 2006.

Chapter 2

1. www.brainyquote.com/quotes/authors/a/albert_einstein.html.
2. www.answers.com/topic/hayward-jeremy-w.

Chapter 3

1. Joe Dispenza, *Evolve Your Brain*, 2008.
2. Rupert Sheldrake, *The Sense of Being Stared At*, 2000.
3. Candace Pert, *Molecules of Emotion*, 1999.
4. *Ibid*.
5. Daniel Monte, *What the Bleep Do We Know?*, 2005.
6. Lee Pulos, *The Biology of Empowerment*, 2005.
7. I was introduced to these facts from lectures given by Dr Bruce Lipton. The graph showing the brainwave activity is the original work of Dr Lipton's and used with his permission. The visual metaphor of the British Houses of Parliament depicting the processing power of the subconscious and conscious minds is adapted with permission from the original work of Dr Lipton.
8. William Tiller, *Some Science Adventures with Real Magic*, 2005.
9. Tor Norretranders, *The User Illusion: Cutting Consciousness Down to Size*, 1999.
10. *Ibid*.

Chapter 4

1. Benjamin Libet, *Mind Time*, 2005.
2. Gerald Zaltman, *How Customers Think: Essential Insights into the Mind of the Market*, 2003.
3. *Nature*, Neuroscience: Unconscious determinants of free decisions in the human brain, April 13, 2008.
4. Carl Jung, *The Psychology of the Unconscious*, 1943.
5. Daniel Wegner, *The Illusion of Conscious Will*, 2003.
6. August Bullock, *The Secret Sales Pitch: An Overview of Subliminal Advertising*, 2004.
7. *Ibid*.
8. *Journal of Psychology*, 1976.
9. Zaltman, *op. cit.*
10. *Ibid*.

Chapter 5

1. William James, *Principles of Psychology*, 1890.
2. Norman Cousins, *Anatomy of an Illness*, 1991.
3. www.wikipedia.com.
4. S. Wolf, The relation of gastric function to nausea in man, *Journal of Clinical Investigation*, 1943, 22(6): 877–82 [PubMed].
5. *Ibid*.
6. http://www.skeptic.com/eskeptic/09-05-20/.
7. Ellen J. Langar, *Counterclockwise: Mindful Health and the Power of Possibility*, 2010.
8. Joseph Dispenza, *Evolve Your Brain*, 2008.
9. Langar, *op. cit.*
10. *New England Journal of Medicine*, 2002.
11. *Placebo: Mind over Medicine*, Discovery Channel, 2002.
12. Dawson Church, *The Genie in Your Genes: Epigenetic Medicine and the New Biology of Intention*, 2007.
13. *Ibid*.
14. www.drdavidhamilton.com/Articles.
15. Gardiner Morse, The nocebo effect, www.Hippocrates.com, November 1999.

13. *Ibid.*
14. *Ibid.*
15. James L. Oschman, *Energy Medicine: The Scientific Basis*, 2000.
16. Church, *op. cit.*
17. http://www.acupunctureresearch.org.uk/papers/FS6_depression.pdf.

Chapter 8

1. Carl Jung, *Man and His Symbols*, 1997.
2. Ervin Laszlo, *Science and the Akashic Field: An Integral Theory of Everything*, 2007.
3. www.brainyquote.com/quotes/authors/a/albert_einstein.html.
4. Amit Goswami, *The Self-Aware Universe: How Consciousness Creates the Material World*, 1993.
5. Dean Radin, *Entangled Minds*, 2006.
6. *New Scientist*, March 2004.
7. Radin, *op. cit.*
8. *Star Wars*, Lucas Film, 1977.
9. Rupert Sheldrake, *The Sense of Being Stared At, and Other Aspects of the Extended Mind*, 2004.
10. Radin, *op. cit.*
11. Quantum Communication, Intention Media, 2009.
12. Rupert Sheldrake, *The Presence of the Past: Morphic Resonance and the Habits of Nature*, 2000.
13. Pavlov, 1923.
14. Sheldrake, *The Presence of the Past*.
15. *Ibid.*
16. www.klinghardtneurobiology.com/BiophotonPhysics.pdf.
17. *Journal of Subtle Energies and Energy Medicine*, vol. 16, no. 30.
18. David Sereda, *The Voice Movie*, Intention Media, 2008.
19. William A. Tiller and Walter E. Dibble, Jr, *A Brief Introduction to Intention-Host Device Research*, www.Tiller.org.
20. William Tiller, *Psychoenergetic Science*, 2007.
21. *Ibid.*
22. Radin, *op. cit.*
23. *Ibid.*

24. Dean Radin, *The Noetic Universe*, 2009.
25. Radin, *Entangled Minds*.
26. *Ibid.*
27. Results of the National Demonstration Project, June–July, 1993, *Social Indicators Research*, 1999 47: 153–201.

Chapter 9

1. Nick Begich, Interview 3, www.consciousmedianetwork.com.
2. Clare Graves, *The Never Ending Quest*, 2005.
3. Ervin Laszlo and Jude Currivan, *Cosmos*, 2008.
4. Ken Wilber, *Integral Life Practice Starter Kit*, 2006.
5. http://diabetes.about.com/lw/Health-Medicine/Conditions-and-diseases/Diabetes-and-Strength-Training.htm.
6. Wilber, *op. cit.*

Chapter 10

1. The Mind–Body Belief-Change process that you will learn in this book is an outgrowth of the work of Dr Paul Dennison who created Educational Kinesiology (Edu-K) and Rob Williams who created the PSYCH-K® process. My belief-change process simplifies and extends this work by adding the information from neurocardiology and specifically the heart–brain connection and the understanding that checking a belief change process is 100% integrated is a crucial step in making sure the change is comprehensive.
2. Association for Comprehensive Energy Psychology, 2005 Conference.
3. Deitrich Klinghardt, Psycho-NeuroBiology Workshop, Seattle, 2001.
4. *Journal of Perceptual and Motor Skills*, 1999.
5. William Tiller, *Psychoenergetic Science*, 2007.
6. *Ibid.*
7. John Diamond, *Your Body Doesn't Lie*, 1985.

Chapter 11

1. Fritjof Capra, *The Tao of Physics: An Exploration of the Parallels between Modern Physics and Eastern Mysticism*, 2000.
2. Bruce Lipton, As above so below: An introduction to fractal evolution, lecture, The Seventh International Conference on Science & Consciousness, April 2006.
3. www.brainyquote.com/quotes/authors/m/max_planck.html.
4. *Nature*, The immaterial universe, July 2005.
5. Deepak Chopra, *The New Physics of Healing*, 2001.
6. Claude Swanson, *The Synchronised Universe: New Science of the Paranormal*, 2003.
7. *Ibid.*
8. *Ibid.*
9. William James, *The Varieties of Religious Experience*, 1902.
10. Marilyn Schlitz, Cassandra Vieten and Tina Amorok, *Living Deeply: The Art and Science of Transformation in Everyday Life*, 2008.
11. Mouni Sadhu, *In Days of Great Peace*, 2001.

Appendix A

1. *Mail on Sunday*, August 8, 2004.
2. *The Voice Movie*, Intention Media, 2008.
3. Rupert Sheldrake, *The Sense of Being Stared At, and Other Aspects of the Extended Mind*, 2004.
4. *Ibid.*
5. Claude Swanson, *The Synchronised Universe: New Science of the Paranormal*, 2003.
6. Ayahuasca, neurogenesis and depression, www.ayahuasca.com.
7. Marilyn Schlitz, Cassandra Vieten and Tina Amorok, *Living Deeply: The Art and Science of Transformation in Everyday Life*, 2008.

ABOUT THE AUTHOR

Chris is an internationally recognised performance psychologist. He runs Gamma Healing public workshops, organisational training and coaching programmes and has trained world champion athletes. He is a visiting lecturer at the University of Westminster Business School and is a sought-after keynote speaker. He is also the author of:

Peak Performance in 60 Seconds

The 4 Essentials to Maximise Your Energy, Resilience and Business Performance

Feel free to contact Chris anytime:
Chris@ChrisWaltonUK.com
www.ChrisWaltonUK.com
07951 043053

CPSIA information can be obtained at www.ICGtesting.com
Printed in the USA
LVOW101535300512

283960LV00007B/6/P